NEW ME

*She Stoops
to Co*

NEW MERMAIDS

General editor: Brian Gibbons
Professor of English Literature, University of Münster

Reconstruction of an eigthteeth-century stage
by C.Walter Hodges

NEW MERMAIDS

Goldsmith, after the portrait by Reynolds, 1770.

Oliver Goldsmith

She Stoops to Conquer

2nd edition

edited by James Ogden

Formerly Senior Lecturer in English
University of Wales, Aberystwyth

A & C Black • London
WW Norton • New York

Second edition 2001
A & C Black (Publishers) Limited
37 Soho Square
London W1D 3QZ

ISBN 0 7136 5086 9

© 2001 A & C Black (Publishers) Limited

First New Mermaid edition 1979
Ernest Benn Limited

Published in the United States of America
by W. W. Norton & Company Inc.
500 Fifth Avenue, New York, NY 10110

ISBN 0-393-90092-4

CIP catalogue records for this book are available from the British Library and
the Library of Congress.

Printed in Great Britain by
Bookmarque Ltd, Croydon, Surrey

CONTENTS

To Lavinia and Rachel

ACKNOWLEDGEMENTS

I am grateful to the Huntington Library, San Marino, California, for providing a microfilm of the Larpent manuscript of *She Stoops to Conquer*. For other assistance with research I am grateful to the staffs of the National Library of Wales and the Aberystwyth University Library, and to my friends Richard Brinkley, Anne Gardiner, and David Shuttleton. For constructive criticism I am much indebted to the General Editor, Brian Gibbons, and my friend Tom Craik. And my debts to previous editors, especially Tom Davis and Arthur Friedman, must not be left in the obscurity of learned footnotes. Presentation was much improved by the work of Sue Gibbons and Katie Taylor. Everything benefited from my wife's steady support and my daughter's sparkling comments.

INTRODUCTION

The Author

Goldsmith outlined his ancestry and early life for his official biographer, who did not wholly believe him. He told Thomas Percy he was descended from a Spanish family which came to England in the reign of Queen Mary I. One of them married a Miss Goldsmith, taking the name and – presumably – the Protestant side. Recent forbears were clergymen in the Anglican Church of Ireland; his father was a country vicar, and his mother the daughter of an ordained schoolmaster. There were seven children, of whom Goldsmith was the fourth, born at Pallas, Co. Longford, on 10 November 1730 or 1731 – he was unsure of the year – and named after Oliver Cromwell. Percy believed he was born in 1728 and named after his maternal grandfather, but modern biographers have thought 1731 the most likely year, and shown that his mother's family were supporters of Cromwell. Percy was not told that as a boy Goldsmith had smallpox, which left him permanently marked and painfully self-conscious. He attended local schools, and was soon known as an odd mixture of cleverness and folly.[1]

Goldsmith was at Trinity College, Dublin, from 1745 to 1750, when he became a Bachelor of Arts. He hated his tutor, and 'made no great figure in mathematics', but 'could turn an Ode of Horace into English better than any of them'.[2] Meanwhile his father had died, and for some years he relied for moral and financial support on a comparatively wealthy clerical uncle. He considered various careers: the church, law, teaching, even emigration to America. In 1752 he went to Edinburgh to study medicine, and in 1754 to Leiden in search of better tuition. Although he later practised as a physician, claimed he was a Bachelor of Medicine, and became known as Dr Goldsmith, it is doubtful if he ever took a medical degree.[3] From Leiden he set off on a walking tour of the Netherlands, France, Switzerland and Italy, perhaps making money

---

[1] Percy's 'Memoir' in Goldsmith's *Miscellaneous Works* (1801) incorporated his 'Memorandum' of a conversation with the author, and a letter from his sister, Mrs Catherine Hodson. Both are reprinted in E. H. Mikhail, ed., *Goldsmith: Interviews and Recollections* (Macmillan, 1993).

[2] Quoted by John Forster, *Life of Goldsmith* (1848) ch. ii, and mentioned by Ralph M. Wardle, *Oliver Goldsmith* (Kansas University Press, 1957) p. 31.

[3] Percy was sceptical, and Garrick jokes about Goldsmith's medical qualifications; see below, 'Prologue' ll. 31–46.

by playing the flute at peasant gatherings, or saving expenses by seeking the hospitality of Irish convents. In Paris he apparently saw fine performances of Molière's *L'Avare* and *Le Médecin Malgré Lui*.[4] In 1756 he reached London, which he made his home.

Finding no money in medicine, Goldsmith turned to literature, and for the rest of his life he was rarely without hack work. He was well paid for such major efforts as the *History of England*, the *Grecian History*, the *Roman History*, and the *History of the Earth, and Animated Nature*, but gambling, extravagance in dress, and excessive generosity kept him in debt. More original work began with his ambitious *Enquiry into the Present State of Learning in Europe* (1759) and *The Bee* (also 1759), a weekly magazine which included some of his best essays. Another series of essays was published as *The Citizen of the World* (1762). By this time Dr Johnson considered him one of the best English authors, and with Johnson and Sir Joshua Reynolds he was one of the founders of the exclusive Turk's Head Club. He became well known as a poet with *The Traveller* (1764), and still more with *The Deserted Village* (1770), poems lamenting rural decay in the face of commercial development. He also pleased himself, his critical friends, and his public with the novel *The Vicar of Wakefield* (1766) and the comedies *The Good-Natured Man* (1768) and *She Stoops to Conquer* (1773). Johnson, though well aware of his friend's intellectual, conversational and social failings, told Reynolds and Boswell: 'Whether we take him as a poet, as a comic writer, or as an historian, he stands in the first class'.[5] Probably he said nothing so flattering in his presence, and on 4 April 1774 Goldsmith shocked everyone by his sudden death. He was suffering from kidney disease, much aggravated by his own inappropriate treatment.

Goldsmith was not ashamed of his origins, and kept his Irish brogue, which to some people seemed to betray 'low' social status. But he grew estranged from his mother, and did not attend her funeral. Indeed he never returned to Ireland, though he never truly settled in England, and never married. He knew his own merits, wanted to be taken seriously, and at times seemed conceited; he also knew his own failings, could not take himself seriously, and at times seemed foolish. As Johnson said, he had no settled notions, and tended 'to blurt out whatever was on his mind, and see what would become of it'.[6] But if his chatter was sometimes naïve or incoherent, it was generally meant to amuse or inspire. His appearance and conversation got him nowhere with the ladies:

---

[4] 'Remarks on our Theatres', *The Bee* (1759); *Works*, vol. I pp. 359–63.

[5] Boswell, 30 April 1773; p. 527.

[6] Boswell, 9 April 1778; p. 917.

When in company with ladies he was always endeavouring after humour, and as continually failed; but his ill success was equally diverting to the company as if he had succeeded. If they laughed, he was happy and did not seem to care whether it was with him or at him.[7]

It is easy to understand why he did not *seem* to care, but hard to believe that he did not care. As a student in Edinburgh he invested in a blue satin coat and attended an Assembly, but did not enjoy it, and concluded that 'an ugly and a poor man is society only for himself'.[8] In 1770 he accompanied Mrs Hannah Horneck and her pretty daughters Catherine and Mary on a visit to Paris, but they all quickly tired of his efforts to amuse them. Biographers have speculated that he was in love with Mary, but if he indulged such a feeling, he hardly expected much response. He got on much better with lower-middle-class ladies like Mrs Butler, who was for a while his landlady, or the Misses Gunn, who sometimes altered his clothes. He also knew some less respectable ladies; Johnson remarked that occasionally when drunk Goldsmith would go in a coach with 'a little whore or so', and boast about it afterwards.[9]

Isaac D'Israeli imagined Goldsmith comparing himself with Johnson: he might have preferred his own spontaneity to Johnson's deliberation; the elegance of his poems to the severity of Johnson's; the homely descriptions of *The Vicar of Wakefield* to the exotic fancies of *Rasselas*; his own 'original humour' in comedy to Johnson's 'turgid declamations' in tragedy. 'Goldsmith therefore, without any singular vanity, might have concluded from his own reasonings, that he was not an inferior writer to Johnson'. Unfortunately their contemporaries concluded otherwise, so Goldsmith acquired a reputation for ridiculous self-importance.[10] But Johnson himself was generally fair to his friend's character and achievements. He wrote to Boswell: 'He died of a fever, made, I am afraid, more violent by uneasiness of mind'. He owed perhaps £2000 – 'Was ever poet so trusted before?' He told another correspondent: 'Let not his frailties be remembered: he was a very great man'. Later Johnson composed the Latin epitaph for Goldsmith's monument in Westminster Abbey, emphasising that he touched almost all kinds

---

[7] Frederick W. Hilles, ed., *Portraits by Sir Joshua Reynolds* (Heinemann, 1952) pp. 48–9.

[8] *Letters*, p. 9

[9] Boswell, *Journal of a Tour to the Hebrides*, ed. F. A. Pottle and Charles W. Bennett (New York, 1936) pp. 344–5; John Ginger, *The Notable Man* (Hamish Hamilton, 1977) pp. 286–7.

[10] Isaac D'Israeli, *Miscellanies* (1796) pp. 30–33.

of writing, and none that he did not adorn: 'nullum quod tetigit non ornavit'.[11]

The Play: Context and Sources

Goldsmith wrote forcefully about the theatre of his time. He appreciated Mlle. Clairon's tragic gestures on the Parisian stage, and Ned Shuter's comic business at Covent Garden, but thought such excellent acting unusual.[12] He argued that although 'our stage is more magnificent than any other in Europe', its managers yielded to the demands of critics, actors and audiences for bombastic tragedy, genteel comedy, and mere spectacle, so it was unlikely that self-respecting authors would 'turn to the stage for either fame or subsistence'.[13] But he was a natural dramatist, as many passages in his prose works may suggest: the discordant meeting of the Harmonical Society, the dialogue of Altangi the Chinese philosopher and Fudge the London bookseller, or the characterisation of Beau Tibbs.[14] So maybe more for subsistence than fame he wrote *The Good-Natured Man*, moving the beau to the stage as the self-important Lofty. This comedy played successfully enough at Covent Garden, but a scene of 'low' comedy – in which the hero is bothered by bailiffs – was hissed and had to be cut, while audiences preferred Hugh Kelly's much more genteel *False Delicacy* at Drury Lane. In his preface to the printed text Goldsmith maintained that genteel comedy, which represented high life, supported conventional morality, and discouraged hearty laughter, was unknown to 'the poets of the last age'; he has imitated them, has offered a wider range of characters than usual, and has included more really funny scenes. But compared with *She Stoops to Conquer*, *The Good-Natured Man* is too clever, complicated, and stagey.

Before the first performance of his second comedy Goldsmith wrote another 'Essay on the Theatre', in which he contrasted 'the weeping sentimental comedy' which was currently fashionable, with 'the laughing and even low comedy' which had formerly flourished. He would have us believe that the former is 'a species of bastard tragedy', while the latter is true comedy as defined by Aristotle. These assertions should not be taken too seriously. It was true that

---

[11] Boswell, letters of 4 and 5 July 1774, epitaph, May 1776; pp. 563–5, 778–9.

[12] 'Remarks on our Theatres' and 'On our Theatres', *The Bee* (1759); *Works*, vol. I pp. 359–63 and 389–91.

[13] 'Upon Criticism' and 'Of the Stage', *An Enquiry into the Present State of Learning in Europe* (1759); *Works*, vol. I pp. 317–30.

[14] 'A Description of Various Clubs', *Busy Body* (1759); *Works*, vol. III pp. 11–13. *The Citizen of the World* (1762); *Works*, vol. II pp. 213–17, 225–476 *passim*.

comedy had tended to displace tragedy on the London stage, but not that this comedy was mostly sentimental. Here of course are problems of definition: we can distinguish laughing from sentimental comedy if we have to think only of *The Country Wife* (1675) and *The Country Girl* (1766), but between such extremes all is debatable. The success of Garrick's adaptation, which drove Wycherley's original from the stage till the twentieth century, shows that there was a fashion for sentimental comedy. And arguably there is some sentimentalism in any play, *The Good-Natured Man* for example, in which a flawed hero more or less reforms and gets the girl and the money. But scholars and critics have sometimes made the fashion seem more influential or deplorable than it really was or is. Now we have very full records of the stage between Goldsmith's arrival in London and his publication of this essay, we can perhaps agree that laughing comedy was at least as popular as weeping. The essay emerges as a journalistic piece, or puff theoretical, provoked by the alarming success of Richard Cumberland's genteel comedies in the 1772–3 season, and intended to prepare audiences for *She Stoops to Conquer*.[15]

Goldsmith hints at a literary source for the play when Kate, the heroine, wonders if she looks like Cherry in *The Beaux' Stratagem* (III.i.231–3). In Farquhar's comedy (1707), two beaux tour the provinces to find ladies and fortune; one of them, who pretends to be a footman, thinks of seducing Cherry, a barmaid. In Goldsmith's, two beaux go down to the country to meet ladies honourably; one of them thinks of seducing Kate, who pretends to be a barmaid. A more likely source is Marivaux's *Le Jeu de l'Amour et du Hasard* (1730). Here our scene is Paris, where Orgon, a gentleman, has arranged for Silvia, his daughter, to marry Dorante, the son of an old friend. Knowing that Dorante is to meet her disguised as his valet, he agrees to let Silvia meet him disguised as her maid; both hope to find out if they love each other, but are surprised to find themselves falling for their supposed social inferiors. The play becomes mainly an exploration of the heroine's character, because Dorante explains who he is and proposes marriage, but Silvia does not explain who she is or accept him till she has tested him further. Meanwhile the real servants also fall in love and enact a parody of bourgeois romance. Goldsmith may have known the play, as there are verbal parallels,[16]

---

[15] 'An Essay on the Theatre', *Westminster Magazine* (1773); *Works*, vol. III pp. 209–13. Robert D. Hume, 'Goldsmith and Sheridan and the Supposed Revolution of "Laughing" against "Sentimental" Comedy', in Paul J. Korshin, ed., *Studies in Change and Revolution* (Scolar, 1972) pp. 237–76, using evidence from *The London Stage*, maintains that laughing comedy was the more popular, but his findings have not been fully accepted.

[16] Arthur Lytton Sells, *Les Sources Françaises de Goldsmith* (Paris, 1924) pp. 156–61.

and Silvia's masquerade may be the source for Kate's. But if he did, he has cut the father's complicity in the plot, made the play at least equally an exploration of the hero's character, and added many farcical complications, especially in the subplot for the heroine's mother, stepbrother, and another pair of lovers.

Sources for the stepbrother, Tony Lumpkin, have been found in Jerry in Wycherley's *Plain Dealer* (1676), Young Hartford in Shadwell's *Lancashire Witches* (1681), Johnny in Cibber's *Woman's Wit* (1697), Humphry Gubbin in Steele's *Tender Husband* (1705), Timothy in the anonymous *The Lottery* (1731), Hodge in Bickerstaffe's *Love in a Village* (1762), and elsewhere. The length of the list suggests the hazards of source-hunting. John Harrington Smith discusses all these except Hodge, and John Ginger says Hodge is 'of course, the literary progenitor of Tony Lumpkin'.[17] Smith concludes more cautiously that a dramatist knowing all the antecedent country boobies would suppose that the type should be fond of hunting, drinking, and low company; he would play jokes on his mother, but would be her pride and joy; she might try to marry him to his cousin, but he might help the girl to marry the man of her choice. Hence Lumpkin's character and adventures are typical, and Goldsmith probably knew some of these sources. Ginger argues that Bickerstaffe borrowed the lovers disguised as servants from Marivaux, but moved them to the country, and added the second love affair and the rustic servant Hodge. Goldsmith turned Hodge into young Squire Lumpkin and emphasised his stormy relationship with his mother. But despite 'the exceptionally high level of literary plagiarism' Ginger finds in *She Stoops to Conquer*, he admits that 'one is still left with a strong impression of creativeness and originality'.

In a comprehensive and critical account of all proposed sources, Susan Hamlyn concludes that the influence of Marivaux and Bickerstaffe has been exaggerated, though the play can be seen as a new mixture of traditional ingredients.[18] After all, some resemblance to *The Beaux' Stratagem* must have been seen immediately by Reynolds, who proposed titling the play *The Belle's Stratagem*.

The Play: A Commentary

Now we can join that London audience of 1773. Our scene is Hardcastle's old-fashioned house deep in the English countryside.

[17] Smith, 'Tony Lumpkin and the Country Booby Type in Antecedent English Comedy', *PMLA* 58 (1944) 1038–49; Ginger (note 9), p. 299.

[18] *She Stoops to Conquer: The Making of a Popular Success* (MA thesis, Birmingham University, 1975) ch. 1.

Only its owner is old-fashioned in appearance; his wife is more or less new-fashioned, his daughter seems to him 'fond of French frippery', and his visitors from London 'look woundily like Frenchmen'. To us Kate Hardcastle, her friend Constance Neville, and their suitors look normal enough. These characters mostly speak and move with an elegance we can admire. Hardcastle's stepson Tony Lumpkin, his drinking companions, and Kate when stooping to conquer, speak and move in ways some of us may think 'low' or rustic; but if so, we may think again. Soon all are involved in farcical mistakes, so we scarcely suppose we are getting a slice of real life, and we may feel transported to a world of theatrical fantasy. For audiences today, this effect may be reinforced by the costumes, scenes and manners of a remote time, place and society. But when we leave the theatre we know we have had to laugh about perennial problems: the nature of gentility, the conflicts of generations, the roles of genders. It may be time to think about them.

She Stoops to Conquer, or The Mistakes of a Night is a well-made play. The opening scene deftly introduces the country characters: the hidebound Hardcastle and his darling daughter Kate; the scheming Mrs Hardcastle, her mischievous son Tony and her nice niece Constance. Hardcastle's old friend Sir Charles Marlow proposes a match between his son and Kate, while Mrs Hardcastle promotes one between her son and Constance. Young Marlow and his friend Hastings come down, Hastings planning to elope with Constance, Marlow expecting to get nowhere with Kate. Tony tricks the visitors into thinking the house is an inn; Marlow casts his prospective father-in-law as the landlord, and his prospective wife as the barmaid; Hardcastle plays his role unconsciously, but threatens to throw Marlow out; Kate plays hers consciously, and promises to reel him in. Tony's schemes to help Constance and Hastings finally determine his mother to keep them apart. The plots are not quite unravelled by Sir Charles's belated arrival and Tony's mischievous masterpiece; both pairs of lovers must understand each other better before there can be happy endings.

The mistakes are made and unmade in a few hours in the theatre, and are supposed to take little longer in real life. The first Act has scenes at the house before Tony goes out for a drink and the ladies take their afternoon walk (I.i.200), and at the alehouse soon afterwards. Three long Acts in the house follow. In Act II the visitors arrive, and a servant brings in candles (61 s.d.). They discuss 'tonight's supper' (257), and Kate returns from her walk still smartly dressed as before. In Act III she is 'plainly dressed' (8 s.d.) to please her father and attract Marlow. By the end of this Act a modern audience will expect the interval. At the beginning of Act IV Sir Charles is expected 'this night', and it is very late when Hardcastle asks Marlow to leave (138–9). Mrs Hardcastle's threatened journey to aunt Pedigree's means going thirty miles 'before morning' (399). Act V begins still in the house two hours later (IV.i.433–4, V.i.9–10), but its three scenes suggest events rushing to a climax. Sir Charles is keen to conclude the match between his son and Kate. The candles are snuffed for Hastings's rendezvous with Tony in the garden, where Hardcastle takes 'one of his night walks' (V.ii.83–4). For the final scene we return to the house, and when all's said and done it is time to think again of supper (V.iii.160). Different backdrops are wanted for the alehouse and garden scenes, but the play's beginning, middle and end all take place in the house. Variety is created by frequent exits and entrances making many combinations of the seven principals, mostly in twos and threes; at IV.i.375–6 when Marlow makes a fourth Tony tells us 'we shall have old Bedlam broke loose presently'. Attention focuses on the two plots alternately.[19] The play needs only a small stage and simple devices, but demands good timing and stylish presentation.

Early critics enjoyed complaining of improbabilities. They thought it unlikely that the visitors would mistake the house for an inn; that Kate would dress plainly when expecting a suitor, and Marlow mistake her for a barmaid; that Hastings and Constance would let him persist in error; that Mrs Hardcastle would start a long journey at midnight; and that she could be fooled into driving for hours in a circle.[20] Defenders of the play said some of these things actually happened: Goldsmith himself mistook his father's friend's house for an inn one evening, and was allowed to behave like a paying guest till morning; his fellow-dramatist Sheridan fooled Mme. de Genlis into driving round for hours and coming back to his house.[21] But such defences cannot lessen the unlikelihood of so many farcical events at one place in a few hours, so Goldsmith took pains to make the plot probable enough in the theatre. We see immediately that Hardcastle's 'old rambling mansion ... looks for all the world like an inn' (I.i.14–15). Tony is obviously mischievous, irritated by his parents, patronised by the Londoners: no wonder he gets the idea of making them think the old house really is an inn. The trick would fail if the supposed landlord introduced himself, so he first meets the visitors offstage, and when we see them together he both knows who they are and thinks they know who he is. For them the idea of an old inn is confirmed by the antique furniture, and of an eccentric landlord by

[19] Main plot: II.i.62–488, III.i.1–84, 224–end, IV.i.19–246, V.i, V.iii.1–98. Sub-plot: II.i.489–end, III.i.85–223, IV.i.1–18, 247–end, V.ii, V.iii.99–150.

[20] William Woodfall, *Monthly Review* 48 (1773) 309–14, in G. S. Rousseau, ed., *Goldsmith: The Critical Heritage* (Routledge, 1974) pp. 115–18.

[21] Thomas Moore, *Memoirs of Sheridan* (2nd ed., 1825) vol. II pp. 192–6.

their old-fashioned welcome. Marlow's mistake over Kate is also carefully prepared. When they first meet she has been out walking and still wears her bonnet, and he is too shy to look her in the face, addressing much of what he says aside to Hastings or the audience. Her father challenges her to dress plainly despite the arrival of her suitor (I.i.99–101), and she needs only a bunch of keys and a rustic accent to be taken for a barmaid. We know he likes barmaids (II.i.102) and she has studied the role in a play (III.i.231–3). Hastings and Constance conspire to keep him in the dark till their elopement plans are complete. When Mrs Hardcastle finds them out she is furious enough to insist on the midnight journey, and if Marlow and Hastings can imagine such places as Crackskull Common, then so can she (I.ii.130, V.ii.67). This nightmare landscape was and is familiar to audiences from Gothic novels and horror films. But in the end Goldsmith relies on us to accept the mistakes and madness of the night for the sake of entertainment. Dr Johnson knew of 'no comedy for many years that has so much exhilarated an audience'.[22] Mrs Inchbald takes us further in understanding the play's permanent appeal:

> *She Stoops to Conquer* has indeed more the quality of farce than of a regular five-act drama: but, although some of the incidents are improbable, there is not one character in the piece, which is not perfectly in nature. The reader will find his country friends in the whole family of the Hardcastles; and, most likely, one of his town acquaintances in the modest Mr Marlow.[23]

Paradoxically, a largely incredible series of events befalls an essentially credible group of characters; which is almost a definition of comedy.

The ages of the main characters cause confusion.[24] Tony is twenty-one (V.iii.137–8); to play him any older would make nonsense of everything. Mrs Hardcastle wants him to marry Constance, who anticipates being free to marry Hastings in two or three years (IV.i.421–3, V.ii.149–50), so she must be about eighteen. Kate implies that she too is eighteen (III.i.293–4), and her father's promise not to enforce marriage would seem pointless if she were much older. The ages of their lovers are less certain. To Hastings Tony seems young (II.i.547, 595, 606–7), so he should seem older, about the same age as Marlow. To Hardcastle Marlow is a young gentleman 'bred a scholar, and designed for an employment in the

---

[22] Boswell, 29 April 1773; p. 525.

[23] *She Stoops to Conquer with Remarks by Mrs Inchbald* (London, *c*. 1808) p. 6.

[24] Davis, p. 58 note, and A. N. Jeffares, *York Notes on She Stoops to Conquer* (Longman, 1980), p. 18, are both misleading.

service of his country' (I.i.115–17). Apparently neither Marlow nor
Hastings has got far in his career. The older generation should be
played as distinctly older, though Mrs Hardcastle minimises her
age, and Hardcastle maximises his. She claims to be forty, and he
says she is fifty-seven (I.i.26–30). An audience will assume she is
lying, and later Hastings assumes she is at least fifty (II.i.537–40).
Hence Hardcastle is probably not yet sixty, but his stories of battles
long ago make him seem older.[25] They have been married long
enough for him to claim he has been 'pretty fond of an old wife'
(I.i.22–3).

The Hardcastles may confirm prejudices about our 'country
friends'. He idolises the country and 'everything that's old', she the
town and everything that's new. She has been married before, and
Tony is her son by her first husband; commentators sometimes
assume he has been married before, and Kate is his daughter by his
first wife. As this assumption is not based on the text, it may be
deduced from the situation: he dotes on his daughter almost as
much as she dotes on her son, so she leaves Kate's affairs to him,
and he leaves Tony's to her. But where he is an amiable match-
maker who will have Kate and Marlow marry only if they agree, she
is a control freak who would make Tony and Constance marry even
though they refuse.

Hardcastle partly understands his wife's relationship with her
son; they are 'a pair that only spoil each other' (I.i.84). He does not
spoil his 'pretty darling', but tells her the young man he has pro-
visionally 'chosen to be your husband' is expected immediately, and
she must decide if she will have him, though 'he may not have *you*'.
She loves her father, does not merely honour him, and if he teases
her tactlessly, she asserts herself respectfully: 'My dear Papa, why
will you mortify one so?' (I.i.103–41). And there is some affection
in his stepson's description of him as 'the old grumbletonian'
(I.ii.74–5). But we really warm to him in his scene with the pro-
moted farmworkers, who are to keep their places, and not laugh at
his jokes:

DIGGORY
    Then ecod your worship must not tell the story of ould Grouse in the
    gun-room: I can't help laughing at that – he! he! he! – for the soul of
    me. We have laughed at that these twenty years – ha! ha! ha!
HARDCASTLE
    Ha! ha! ha! The story is a good one. Well, honest Diggory, you may
    laugh at that   (II.i.34–9)

In relating to servants, Hardcastle's decent old ways are preferable

---

[25] Notes to II.i.165, 177–9, 231.

Act II scene i. Hugh Fraser as Hastings and Betty Marsden as
Mrs Hardcastle in William Gaskill's 1982 production at the
Lyric, Hammersmith. © Chris Pearce/Arena Images

to Hastings and Marlow's supercilious new ones. But an actor should not make him too amiable, as he must be annoyed with his visitors, and must eventually order Marlow out of the house. Marlow's insolent defiance prompts a sarcastic speech and vigorous action from Hardcastle: if this young man thinks he owns the place, let him take the candlesticks, the firescreen, the bellows, even the furniture. But when Marlow's mistake is explained, he is quickly forgiven, and urged not to take the matter too seriously: 'An hour or two's laughing with my daughter will set all to rights again' (V.i.35–6). With his daughter's affairs settled, he finally intervenes to help Tony, claiming rather weakly that he had thought concealment of his age might bring improvement in his character.

If Hardcastle is not beyond criticism, even an audience of feminists might find difficulty in siding with his wife, dolled up to look as young as possible, not seen in a truly affectionate relationship with anyone. She nags her husband, deceives her son, and bullies her niece. She also covets the family fortunes, but she is a creature of impulse, and all her schemes are foiled. Her son's 'agreeable, wild notes' remind her of her late husband, but Tony rightly if ungrammatically advises her that she is 'the wildest of the two' (II.i.589–92; IV.i.284–6). In one mood she will happily marry Tony and Constance tomorrow, and in another she will angrily drive Constance and Hastings apart for three years. She is next seen emerging from a horsepond like a muddy mermaid, and pleading with a supposed highwayman like a loving mother; but as the highwayman is really Hardcastle, we laugh at the absurdity rather than weep with the feeling. That Goldsmith had some sympathy for her is implied by her pungent comment on Constance and Hastings's repentance: 'Pshaw, pshaw, this is all but the whining end of a modern novel' (V.iii.127–8). If psychoanalysis is wanted, we may say loss of youth and beauty has left her sadly insecure; but as her schemes for security are both selfish and unsuccessful, we are likely to see her as a comic villain.

Tony Lumpkin bounds across the drawing room on his way to the alehouse. His mother snobbishly dismisses his drinking companions as 'a low, paltry set of fellows', but to him they are individuals, whatever their status:

> Not so low neither. There's Dick Muggins the exciseman, Jack Slang the horse doctor, little Aminadab that grinds the music box, and Tom Twist that spins the pewter platter. (I.i.74–6)

Can this eloquent rascal make a permanent escape from his satirical father-in-law and possessive mother? The actor playing Tony must not be too old – as happens in professional productions – or questions of motive will arise. He must appear as he does to Hardcastle, 'a mere composition of tricks and mischief', and to

Constance, 'a good-natured creature at bottom' (I.i.39–40, 198). His tricks show he is no fool, but notes his victims' weaknesses: his father-in-law's potential obsequiousness, his mother's blinding obsessions, the visitors' assumed superiority. He is not infallible: he knows 'the difference between jest and earnest' when conducting his mother's mad dances, but not when considering the cock-fighting fraternity's urgent news. Marlow reproaches him for the effects of his folly – 'What might be amusement to you, is here disappointment, and even distress' – so he dreams up another mischievous scheme, with the aim of proving himself 'a more good-natured fellow than you thought for' (IV.i.430–7), and the result of freeing himself to renounce Constance and enjoy his inheritance. Now he can be his own man, or at least a worthy son of a father who 'kept the best horses, dogs and girls in the whole county' (I.ii.54–5). He fancies Bet Bouncer, with 'eyes as black as sloes, and cheeks as broad and red as a pulpit cushion', big enough to make a Constance Neville twice over (II.i.626–30). He suggests that the abundant satisfactions of the country surpass the refined pleasures of the town. Critics see him in Shakespearean roles, though he is too young for Falstaff, too fat for Puck, and too innocent for Caliban. He has a plum role anyway.

Of the play's romantic plots, the sub-plot is the more conventional. As in much period comedy, the lovers' problems are more financial than psychological. Hastings is too hasty to worry about money, but Constance hesitates to elope without her 'little fortune' which 'chiefly consists in jewels'. Such prudence prompts Hastings's romantic if absurd exclamation, 'Perish the baubles! Your person is all I desire' (II.i.333–41). When the baubles are lost but elopement remains possible, fortune, love and prudence are personified:

HASTINGS
Let us fly, my charmer. Let us date our happiness from this very moment. Perish fortune! Love and content will increase what we possess beyond a monarch's revenue. Let me prevail.
MISS NEVILLE
No, Mr Hastings; no. Prudence once more comes to my relief, and I will obey its dictates. In the moment of passion, fortune may be despised, but it ever produces a lasting repentance.   (V.ii.151–9)

Both extremes of sentiment are ridiculous, but the *dénouement* in which the lovers win the approval of Hardcastle and Sir Charles vindicates prudence and provokes cynicism. Avowedly against sentimentalism, Goldsmith admits it to the sub-plot, and Mrs Hardcastle's reference to whining novels expresses but does not eliminate our critical feelings.

But Constance is not an unattractive character. As Tony admits, she is pretty and talented:

> I always loved cousin Con's hazel eyes, and her pretty long fingers, that she twists this way and that, over the haspicholls, like a parcel of bobbins. (IV.i.281–3)

Happily for her, Tony doesn't want her, and Hastings does. To her lover she seems good-tempered, sensible, and quiet – too sensible, when it comes to elopements. Tony claims to know her better:

TONY
> There's not a more bitter cantankerous toad in all Christendom.

HASTINGS (*Aside*)
> Pretty encouragement, this, for a lover!

TONY
> I have seen her since the height of that. She has as many tricks as a hare in a thicket, or a colt the first day's breaking. (II.i.612–17)

Obviously Tony is exaggerating, but possibly Hastings is alarmed; in the 1984 National Theatre production, his assurance faltered here. That Constance has many tricks is proved by her scenes with Tony, above all when she invents the letter about cock-fighting which fools him as well as his mother. She needs all her wits about her, or she will be banished to aunt Pedigree's, where 'constraint and ill-nature' even worse than aunt Hardcastle's awaits her (IV.i.413–14). Determination to keep what little fortune she has may be forgiven in an orphan; it is her dependent situation that makes her comparatively worldly. Characteristically she – unlike Kate – knows all about Marlow.

In the main plot both Tony Lumpkin and financial considerations are cleared out to make room for character study. Kate takes over Tony's mischief, not wanting her first meeting with her suitor to be 'like a thing of business', but knowing herself 'a girl who brings her face to market' (I.i.110–11; III.i.244). Her fortune is small, but Marlow has enough for them both according to his father, who also thinks it high time he married 'a good and virtuous girl' such as Kate (V.i.23–5).[26] Marlow seems indifferent to money, though when he thinks he has fallen for a poor relation he at first feels he must defer to the worldly view that 'the difference of our birth, fortune and education, make an honourable connexion impossible' (IV.i.222–4). But love prevails; he declares with conviction that

---

[26] As Hardcastle has not met Marlow (II.i.144–5), his description of him (I.i.112–34) must derive from Sir Charles's letter (which, in the theatre, he should have in his hand).

Act II scene i. Nigel Terry as Marlow and Tracey Ullman as
Kate Hardcastle in William Gaskill's 1982 production at the
Lyric, Hammersmith. © Chris Pearce/Arena Images

'fortune was ever my smallest consideration', and with prescience
that his father will approve (V.iii.32–3, 42–4). If the course of true
love does not run smooth, that is owing to peculiarities of character: Marlow's certainly, Kate's too perhaps.

There was some dispute over Marlow's credibility. Hazlitt
thought him 'a highly amusing caricature, a ridiculous fancy, but no
more'.[27] But Hazlitt himself could not combine romance and marriage, and other early critics agreed with Mrs Inchbald in recognis-
ing Marlow among their town acquaintances. Constance
immediately warns Kate that 'among women of reputation and
virtue' Marlow is very modest, but 'among creatures of another
stamp' he is quite shameless (I.i.174–7). Kate is not completely horrified, but changes the subject. Marlow's saving grace is that he does
not like himself:

> I'm doomed to adore the sex, and yet to converse with the only part
> of it I despise. This stammer in my address, this awkward prepos-
> sessing visage of mine, can never permit me to soar above the reach
> of a milliner's 'prentice, or one of the duchesses of Drury Lane.
> (II.i.138–42)

Hastings assures him he would succeed with the ladies if he 'could
but say half the fine things to them that I have heard you lavish
upon the barmaid of an inn', but the ladies petrify Marlow: 'to me,
a modest woman, dressed out in all her finery, is the most tremendous object of the whole creation' (101–8). And so it proves on his
first interview with Kate. Hastings does not suffer from such inhi-
bitions, and struggles to understand his friend. It is not as if he lacks
good sense or relevant experience; he has travelled widely, and yet
as they came down from London his 'unaccountable reserve' would
not even let him ask for directions. Marlow says he lacks experience
of high society:

> My life has been chiefly spent in a college, or an inn, in seclusion
> from that lovely part of the creation that chiefly teach men confi-
> dence. I don't know that I was ever familiarly acquainted with a
> single modest woman – except my mother. (II.i.83–7)

You do not need to be a Freudian to infer that Marlow's character
has been determined by his psyche, not his circumstances. The
Freudian explanation might be that some men are so deeply
involved with their mothers that they can neither desire the women
they love, nor love the women they desire.

What's in it for Kate? Her ideal partner must be young and hand-

---

[27] Review in *The Times*, 15 October 1817; *Works*, ed. P. P. Howe, vol. 9 pp. 75–6.

some; it will be an advantage if he is sensible and good-natured; it could be a drawback if he is reserved and sheepish (I.i.149–52). She is herself young, attractive and sophisticated, by night dressing plainly to please her father, by day dressing fashionably to please herself. Marlow has the misfortune to meet her in her finery, but stammers out the sententious speeches he supposes the occasion requires. She finds these ridiculous, but his looks are in his favour – 'we don't meet many such at a horse race in the country' (III.i.65–6) – and he says enough to suggest that 'he has good sense' but lacks self-confidence. When she hears he has mistaken her for a barmaid she seizes the chance of a real meeting with 'one who never addresses any but the wildest of her sex' (III.i.246–7). Like some Shakespearean heroines, she seeks a romantic adventure.

Marlow changes rapidly from avoiding the fine lady to pursuing the supposed barmaid. When Hastings asks if he means to rob the girl of her honour, he replies:

> I don't intend to *rob* her, take my word for it, there's nothing in this
> house I shan't honestly *pay* for.   (IV.i.55–6)

In other words, he treats barmaids as prostitutes. Hastings, alarmed, says 'I believe the girl has virtue', and Marlow says if she has he will certainly not corrupt it. The point of this dialogue may be to assure us that Marlow is not merely a rake, but the effect of it is disturbing nonetheless. The barmaid may not be a lady, 'the most tremendous object of the whole creation', but she is still an object, 'the tempting, brisk, lovely, little thing' (IV.i.43). Kate's problem is now to change him back, from seducer to suitor. Her masquerade has shown that she and Marlow fancy each other, even though Constance's account of him seems correct. Any audience, including an eighteenth-century one, might think mutual attraction a better basis for marriage than parental arrangements. When Marlow realises the house is not an inn, Kate admits she is not a barmaid, but pretends to be a poor relation. Marlow now feels he cannot seduce her, worries about what his father and the world will say, and offers marriage. His love is rewarded by the discoveries that her small fortune does not worry his father, and that she is the woman his father wants for him. There is something sentimental in such an ending, so a mildly cynical modern dramatist wrote a sequel, in which Marlow keeps kissing the maids but so neglects his wife that she has to play a maid again:

> You stooped to conquer you know. You must go on stooping. Go
> and put an apron on at once.[28]

[28] St John Hankin, 'Still Stooping', *Dramatic Sequels* (Secker, 1926) p. 62.

Act V scene iii. Victoria Hasted as Kate Hardcastle and Tom Beard as Young Marlow in Peter Hall's 1993 production at the Queen's Theatre. © Henrietta Butler/Arena Images

Kate duly reappears 'in a print dress, cap and apron', and both arouses Marlow again and pleases her father too. Goldsmith's moral seems to be that girls may have to stoop to conquer, and men behaving badly may wish they would; but women may well think twice about it, and we must all wonder how a marriage like Kate and Marlow's would actually work.

Biographers have seen the author himself in Tony Lumpkin, but there is much of both the author and Tony in Marlow. Probably Goldsmith like Tony loved his mother, later found her impossible, and finally broke free; no doubt he dealt with his guilty feelings by making figures of fun of mothers like Mrs Primrose (in *The Vicar of Wakefield*) and Mrs Hardcastle. But his awkwardness in society and failures with women emerge in Marlow. Tony may represent the man Goldsmith in many ways would have liked to be, and Marlow the man he in some moods feared he was. They are alike in their rejection of ladies and parental pressure, and love of Bet Bouncers and barmaids.

Goldsmith began with objections to sentimentalism, but his play ends with happy marriages in prospect, and everyone pleased except the unsympathetic Mrs Hardcastle. He perhaps expected accusations of hypocrisy, and has tried to complicate the happy ending. When Marlow declares his love, Kate makes sure of her conquest by distrusting his 'pretended rapture' (V.i.106). She wins his implied proposal of marriage and their fathers' blessing, but then '*they retire, she tormenting him*' (V.iii.98 s.d.). Meanwhile Hardcastle is so horrified by his wife's mercenary attitude that he gives Constance and Hastings his blessing too, freeing Tony from any obligation to marry his cousin. Mrs Hardcastle with some justice has recalled the whining end of a novel, and Tony with some asperity offers a parody of the marriage service:

> Witness all men by these presents, that I, Anthony Lumpkin, Esquire, of BLANK place, refuse you, Constantia Neville, spinster, of no place at all, for my true and lawful wife. (V.iii.142–5)

His mother then strikes a discordant note in the chorus of approval:

SIR CHARLES
  Oh brave Squire!
HASTINGS
  My worthy friend.
MRS HARDCASTLE
  My undutiful offspring. (V.iii.148–50)

Marlow and Kate come forward to join the chorus, but she has still not fully agreed to marriage. 'Could I prevail upon my little tyrant here to be less arbitrary', says Marlow, 'I should be the happiest man alive'. Hastings gives Kate further assurance of Marlow's love, and Hardcastle joins their hands; but he has caught the word 'tyrant', and cannot resist a final warning:

> as you have been mistaken in the mistress, my wish is, that you may
> never be mistaken in the wife.   (V.iii.163–4)

So the play ends with a glance at the uneasy relationship with which it began. Predictably this cynical strain is amplified in Goldsmith's epilogue, which not only declares, like most epilogues, that all the world's a stage, but also has Kate imagining herself conquering the town.[29]

Criticism takes literature seriously, and makes *She Stoops to Conquer* tell us that the country must educate the town, children their parents, and women their lovers. But this is above all a play of brilliantly contrived and exceptionally funny scenes: Hardcastle as uncommon innkeeper, Marlow's stammering 'sentimental interview' with Miss Hardcastle, Tony bearing witness to the theft of the jewels, Marlow's servant showing himself sufficiently drunk, Hardcastle becoming himself again but being mistaken by his wife for a highwayman. Many remarks are very funny in their contexts, or can be in the theatre. Hastings encourages his stammering friend: 'Cicero never spoke better'. Mrs Hardcastle asks Hastings what is 'the most fashionable age about town'; he looks at her and suggests it is now fifty; 'Seriously?' – and there must be a pause here – 'Then I shall be too young for the fashion'. Mrs Hardcastle again, having lied to Constance about the loss of the jewels: 'You must learn resignation, my dear.... See me, how calm I am'. Marlow explains to Hastings that he has given the jewels to 'the landlady' for safe keeping: 'To the landlady? – The landlady. – You did! – I did.' This dialogue sets up a good exit line for Hastings: 'May you be as successful for yourself as you have been for me'. Marlow's complacency over his drunken servant – 'the fellow is as drunk as he can possibly be' – leaves the supposed landlord speechless: 'I don't know what you'd have more', says Marlow, 'unless you'd have the poor devil soused in a beer barrel'. Hardcastle tells his wet and muddy wife where she is: 'Don't you remember the horsepond, my dear?' She and many others will remember that.

---

[29] William J. Burling, 'Entrapment in Eighteenth-Century Drama', *Reader Entrapment in Eighteenth-Century Literature*, ed. Carl R. Kropf (AMS Press, 1992) pp. 177–99, argues similarly.

The Play in the Theatre

Goldsmith had problems getting his plays from the study to the stage. Both were approved by his literary friends, and submitted to the managers of the rival theatres, Drury Lane and Covent Garden. But Garrick and Colman could not share his distaste for the current fashion in comedy,[30] had misgivings about both plays, and caused long delays before they were performed. When *The Good-Natured Man* was presented at Covent Garden in 1768, Powell in the leading role of Honeywood was half-hearted, but Shuter and Woodward in the character parts of Croaker and Lofty carried the play. Its reception still made Goldsmith feel it had failed, but there were twelve performances – a respectable number – and three benefit nights brought the author £340. When *She Stoops to Conquer* was accepted for performance at the same theatre in 1773, Colman refused to buy new sets and costumes, the aging Woodward refused to play Tony, more surprisingly 'Gentleman' Smith refused to play Marlow, and in the last week of rehearsals Mrs Catley withdrew from the part of Constance. And there were problems in finding a title and writing an epilogue, which Goldsmith resolved only at the last minute.

For its time, Covent Garden was a very grand theatre. It had a deep backstage for scenic effects, with projecting 'side scenes' to create a vista, and a closed 'back scene' to complete the picture. Its forestage could be reached by doors on either side, projected beyond the proscenium with its painted figures of Tragedy and Comedy, and was the most fully illuminated part of the theatre, where most of a play's action necessarily took place. From here asides or soliloquies were easily thrown away or delivered. The auditorium, with its many side boxes and deep upper and lower galleries, could take at least 1400 spectators.[31] Goldsmith himself, through the eyes of his Chinese philosopher in *The Citizen of the World*, describes a typical audience. 'The order of precedence seemed here inverted', as the poor in the upper gallery seemed masters of the ceremonies, and called for music before the play began. The middle gallery was less riotous, chiefly occupied at this time 'in eating oranges, reading the story of the play, or making assignations'. The pit considered themselves critics, though few knew anything about criticism, so they seemed 'to labour under that restraint which an affectation of superior discernment generally produces'. The wealthy ladies and gentlemen in the boxes continually ogled each other, affecting indifference while burning for conquest, and

[30] See above, 'Context and Sources'.
[31] Allardyce Nicoll, *The Garrick Stage* (Manchester University Press, 1980) pp. 51–8.

so became 'part of the entertainment themselves'. But this satirical observer concludes:

> Upon the whole, the lights, the music, the ladies in their gayest dresses, the men with cheerfulness and expectation in their looks, all conspired to make a most agreeable picture, and to fill a heart that sympathises at human happiness with inexpressible serenity.[32]

For the première of *She Stoops to Conquer* on 15 March 1773 Goldsmith's friends rallied round, and disposed themselves about the theatre, soberly dressed because the court was in mourning for the King of Sardinia. Goldsmith could not bear to watch, but reached the theatre in time to hear a hiss when Mrs Hardcastle emerged from the horsepond. 'What's that?' he asked in alarm. 'Psha! Doctor', croaked Colman, 'don't be fearful of squibs, when we have been sitting these two hours on a barrel of gunpowder'.[33] But the acting had been good enough to raise almost continuous laughter, and not only from the author's friends. One reviewer thought the forced changes to the cast had improved the production:

> Mr Lewes gave most perfect satisfaction to the audience in Mr Marlow. He played the part with ease, with spirit, and with characteristic humour.... Mrs Bulkeley deserved no small share of applause. The author could hardly have wished for a better representative of Miss Hardcastle. Mr Shuter was tolerably perfect, perfectly *sober* and extremely pleasing [as Hardcastle].... Mrs Green was lively and characteristic [as Mrs Hardcastle]. Mr Quick did exceedingly well [as Tony] but had rather too much grimace.[34]

Others remarked on Quick's overacting, but probably his performance improved after the first night. Some years later an experienced theatre critic recalled that 'this comedy was very well acted':

> Lewes played Marlow with the ease of a gentleman; Hardcastle and Tony Lumpkin were supported in a masterly style by Shuter and Quick; so was Miss Hardcastle by Mrs Bulkeley. Mrs Green, in Mrs Hardcastle, maintained her just title to one of the best comic actresses of the age.[35]

---

[32] Letter XXI, *Works* vol. II pp. 89–90.

[33] *European Magazine* 24 (1793) 173.

[34] *The Morning Chronicle*, 16 March 1773; quoted in Hamlyn (note 18) pp. 141–3.

[35] Thomas Davies, *Memoirs of the Life of David Garrick* (3rd ed., 1781) vol. II p. 158.

Act V scene ii. Mr Shuter, Mrs Green and Mr Quick as Mr and
Mrs Hardcastle and Tony Lumpkin. From an anonymous
mezzotint based on a painting by Thomas Parkinson.

There was time for only twelve performances before the end of the season, but three benefit nights brought the author just over £500. During the summer Samuel Foote presented the play six times at the Haymarket, and during the autumn Colman presented it again eight times at Covent Garden. Meanwhile it had played successfully at most towns in England and Ireland, and was said to be 'raising the *laughing standard*' at Paris. Indeed its reception was even wider:

> There is hardly a town in England which boasts a playhouse, or a village which has a theatrical barn in it, where Tony Lumpkin's drolleries have not been ha! ha'd! at this summer. In our American plantations also, has this mirth-exciting comedy been performed. The New York papers ... inform that 'She Stoops to Conquer' was performed at the theatre in John Street, New York, by the American company, on the 2nd of August last.[36]

There is a book to be written on the play's stage history.[37] It has been revived in London over sixty times, at most provincial theatres, by most amateur dramatic societies, and in operatic, musical and film versions. It has proved popular in Ireland, America, France and Germany. The Irish dramatist John O'Keeffe quickly wrote several sequels with such titles as *Tony Lumpkin in Town* (Dublin, 1774). In revivals of the play proper Lumpkin became a vehicle for well-known comedians: Joseph Munden, man of many faces (Haymarket, 1797); Charles Mathews, famous for his one-man shows (Haymarket, 1814); John Liston (Covent Garden, 1817). But in the nineteenth century star actresses often played Kate: Mrs Jordan, whose conquests outside the theatre included the future King William IV (Drury Lane, 1800); Harriet Smithson, who captivated Berlioz (Paris, 1827); Madge Kendal, aged twenty-one (Standard, 1869), and in many other revivals; Ellen Terry (Haymarket, 1874), with Charles Wyndham as Marlow; Marie Litton (Imperial, 1879), a performance that ran for 137 nights; Lillie Langtry on her brilliant début (Haymarket, 1881). Mrs Langtry showed she was a good actress as well as a great beauty, playing the barmaid as a well-bred country girl might have done (*The Times*). Apart from Charles Kemble (Covent Garden, 1817) and a youngish Henry Irving (Queen's, 1869), star actors did not often play Marlow, and when Charles Wyndham took the part again aged fifty-three (Criterion, 1890) he was damned for resembling 'the experienced man-about-town' and reducing the comedy to French farce (*The Times*). Irving gave 'perfect satisfaction' as

---

[36] *The Morning Chronicle*, 8 September 1773; quoted with other reports in *Works* vol. V p. 92.

[37] Hamlyn (note 18) gives much basic information, pp. 210–16.

Marlow but was upstaged by Lionel Brough as Lumpkin, showing he could shine in 'low comedy parts of a superior class' (*The Era*). Brough played Lumpkin till he was well over fifty, and passed on his accumulated gags and routines to his son Sydney, who at the Waldorf in 1906 reproduced them in a 'hearty and hilarious' revival (*The Era*).[38]

In the twentieth century, attempts were made to remove the layers of farce and reveal the original comedy. At the Haymarket in 1909, according to *The Athenaeum*, the company was divided, those of the old school cheerfully bent on buffoonery, those of the new hesitantly reaching for refinement. During the inter-war years, the play was regularly revived at the Old Vic under Lilian Baylis's management. As played by Andrew Leigh, Lumpkin was a slim young man in a smart riding suit, who could be mistaken for an undergraduate on vacation, and who 'might quite conceivably have married Cousin Constance' (*The Era*). A series of delicious Kates – Sybil Thorndike, Edith Evans and Peggy Ashcroft – made these productions highly acceptable despite difficulties with Marlow; Baliol Holloway, for example, seemed too old for Edith Evans. In 1928 and 1930 Sir Nigel Playfair included the play in his series of classic English comedies at the Lyric, Hammersmith. More than usual effort was made to impose a style, with attractive eighteenth-century costumes and sets, much bowing and curtseying, and Aminadab's genteel tunes (I.ii.45–6) if not Aminadab himself. Hardcastle's house had so many books that Marlow could not have mistaken it for an inn, and his garden so much statuary that Mrs Hardcastle could not have mistaken it for Crackskull Common. Sir Nigel yielded to criticism and later played the garden scene effectively but not authentically in total darkness. There was some reaction against his refinements in other productions. In 1932 at the Fortune 'The Representative English Players' grossly overdid the clowning in Lumpkin's scenes, and according to *The Times* there was 'ugly rough and tumble' in Marlow's scenes with Kate. In 1933 at the Old Vic comedy and farce were partly separated: Peggy Ashcroft kept Marlow in order, Roger Livesey was a Puckish Lumpkin with an amiable Bet Bouncer, and young Marius Goring was an amusing Aminadab with a lively bear.

Some distinguished directors have seemed embarrassed by the play, and have had mixed reviews. Donald Wolfit at the Westminster in 1935 'imposed no particular style upon the company' (*The Times*), though as Marlow he set quite a good example. Tyrone Guthrie and his company at the Old Vic in 1939 perhaps tried too hard; Ursula Jeans as Kate entered fully into the

[38] J. P. Wearing, *The London Stage* (Scarecrow Press, 14 vols., 1981–93) gives details of London productions 1900–59, and references to reviews.

role of barmaid, but forgot she was Miss Hardcastle; John Mills as Marlow was suitably handsome and dashing, but excessively 'facetious and up-to-date' (*New Statesman*). Michael Benthall at the New Theatre in 1949 would not let Goldsmith speak for himself, but made his actors first pose, and then act, as caricatures from Rowlandson cartoons. Michael Redgrave still gave a superb performance as Marlow, with a disarming stammer, but Nigel Stock's Lumpkin was reminiscent more of Caliban than Puck, and Angela Baddeley's Mrs Hardcastle 'played to her own make-up' (*The Times*). She started a fashion for highly absurd Mrs Hardcastles, sometimes played by well-known comédiennes. Douglas Seale at the Old Vic in 1960 cast Peggy Mount as Mrs Hardcastle and the pop singer Tommy Steele as her son; Steele's rackety Lumpkin ensured large audiences, but Judi Dench's impish Kate was the real success. At the Garrick in 1969 Braham Murray produced a Mrs Hardcastle so grotesque, and a Hardcastle so grave, that it was difficult to believe they were married; indeed one reviewer called her Mrs Lumpkin. But farce and comedy were again kept apart, and the scenes between Marlow and Kate were done very nicely. Tom Courtenay made you feel that Marlow's assaults on barmaids had been worse in intention than effect, and Juliet Mills that Kate's understanding of him was immediate.

Opinions of productions are influenced by knowing too much or too little of what to expect. In recent reviews, mistakes about the play itself are more frequent – the worst was a confusion of the two pairs of lovers. And disagreements between reviewers are more extreme – what seems 'crudely conceived' to one appears 'definitive' to another. The psychological interest of Marlow is more often remarked on, and the women characters excite more attention. Several reviewers said that in William Gaskill's production at the Lyric in 1982 Betty Marsden's Mrs Hardcastle was unusually sympathetic, but Tracey Ullman's Kate promised to replicate her mother; there was something of Lady Bracknell and Gwendolen about them. But two 1989 productions suggested that sympathy for Mrs Hardcastle should not be insisted on: at the Royal Exchange, Manchester, Una Stubbs made her too young and 'not awful enough', while at the Crucible, Sheffield, Janet Henfrey made her 'as disruptive to the play's comic conclusion as Malvolio is to *Twelfth Night*'s' (quotations from *The Daily Telegraph*) – too disruptive, I would have thought. More simply farcical interpretations did not wholly please either. In Giles Block's 1984 National Theatre production Dora Bryan's Mrs Hardcastle and Tony Haygarth's Lumpkin reminded reviewers of pantomime dames and Buttons. This tendency evidently went further in Peter Wood's 1992 Chichester Festival show, with a hurdy-gurdy boy, grouse shooting, and a Jack-and-the-Beanstalk backdrop. The play was not quite lost, as Dennis Quilley's dignified and hence comic Hardcastle showed

Act V scene ii. Miriam Margolyes as Mrs Hardcastle and David
Essex as Tony Lumpkin in Peter Hall's 1993 production at the
Queen's Theatre. © Henrietta Butler/Arena Images

how it should be done. Peter Hall's 1993 production at the Queen's was received much more favourably. The lovers could have been more interesting, David Essex's Lumpkin was too old – but as one reviewer said, 'Lumpkin is *always* too old' – and the show was stolen by Donald Sinden as a growling Hardcastle and Miriam Margolyes as his richly eccentric wife; but it left no doubt that *She Stoops to Conquer* is 'a mellow, humane, reflective study in self-discovery, with strong Shakespearean echoes' (*The Guardian*) and 'one of the great glories of the British comic tradition' (*The Daily Telegraph*).[39]

Note on the Text

The earliest text is a manuscript prepared before the first performance for the licenser of plays, now in the Larpent Collection at the Huntington Library (L). The earliest printed text is a quarto published soon after the first performance (Q). It sold well – in the theatre on 25 March 1773 'almost everyone present had the play in their hands' – and rapidly ran through six impressions. The first was rushed into print in two different printing shops, with consequent mistakes and inconsistencies; the second largely corrects and regularises these.[40] But Goldsmith neither wrote L nor supervised Q through the press, and there are some ninety differences in wording between them.

An editor must choose a copy text, to be followed in matters indifferent, like whether London should keep 'its fools' (L) or 'its own fools' (Q) at home (I.i.7–8). One may be guided by ideas of the play as originally written or as first performed; I prefer the latter, seeing the play as the outcome of collaboration between author and theatre. So my copy text is the second impression of Q, which is generally closer than L to what was said on the stage; for examples, Q's italicised words and phrases indicate theatrical emphasis, and Marlow's sarcasm (I.ii.97), 'We wanted no ghost to tell us that' (Q), is more theatrical than 'We did not want any body to tell us that' (L). However, as the previous New Mermaid editor Tom Davis argued, Q is sometimes *less* theatrical than L, and some readings of L reappear in later printed texts which claim to give the play as performed, and even to derive from the prompt-books.[41] Hence like

[39] For recent reviews, see *Theatre Record*, 2 (1982) 438–40, 464; 4 (1984) 1022, 1094; 9 (1989) 733, 912, 1751; 12 (1992) 1062–6, 1359–60; 13 (1993) 1230–34; 14 (1994) 827–8.

[40] Davis, p. xxiii; William B. Todd, 'The First Editions of *The Good-Natured Man* and *She Stoops to Conquer*', *Studies in Bibliography* 11 (1958) 133–42.

[41] Tom Davis and Susan Hamlyn, 'What do we do when two Texts differ? *She Stoops to Conquer* and Textual Criticism', in René Wellek and Alvaro Ribiero, eds., *Evidence in Literary Scholarship* (Oxford, Clarendon Press, 1979) pp. 263–79.

Davis I have included more L readings than usual. Unlike him, I sometimes argue that these texts (Bell, Inchbald, Cooke) support Q against L; for examples, see notes to I.ii.123, II.i.427, IV.i.220 and 274, V.iii.86.

In this edition all verbal alterations of Q, and some L readings which are possible or interesting, are recorded in footnotes. All editorial stage-directions are placed in square brackets. Neither Q nor L is wholly reliable for spelling, punctuation and other details, so these are modernised according to New Mermaid conventions. Dashes, indicative of theatrical pauses, are retained but standardised in length; an editor cannot dictate the length of a pause to an actor. The commentary aims at making both the text and its presentation as intelligible to a modern audience as they were to the one Goldsmith and his actors knew.

FURTHER READING

Sources and analogues make the most entertaining and instructive reading. Pierre Marivaux's *Le Jeu de l'Amour et du Hasard* is available in Classiques Larousse and (in a modern English translation) Penguin Classics. Farquhar's *The Beaux' Stratagem*, ed. Michael Cordner, is in the New Mermaids. Scholarly and critical works can be recommended with the proviso that it is best to read several, and consider how far different views can be reconciled.

Editions

She Stoops to Conquer (Scolar Press, 1979). Facsimile of Q.

Collected Works of Oliver Goldsmith, ed. Arthur Friedman (Oxford, Clarendon Press, 1966). In 5 vols., vol. V including *The Good-Natured Man* and *She Stoops to Conquer*. Old spelling.

Oliver Goldsmith: Plays and Poems, ed. Tom Davis (London, Dent; Totowa, N.J., Rowman and Littlefield, 1975). 'Everyman' series; modernised spelling.

Biography and Criticism

Bevis, Richard, *The Laughing Tradition* (Georgia University Press, 1980). Reassessment of 'sentimental' and 'laughing' comedy; includes an appreciation of *She Stoops to Conquer*.

Brooks, Christopher K., 'Goldsmith's Feminist Drama: *She Stoops to Conquer*', *Papers on Language and Literature*, vol. 28 (1992) 38–51.

Burling, H. J., 'Entrapment in Eighteenth-Century Drama', in *Reader Entrapment in Eighteenth-Century Literature*, ed. Carl R. Kropf (New York, AMS Press, 1992), pp. 177–99.

Dixon, Peter, *Oliver Goldsmith Revisited* (Boston, Twayne, 1991). 'Twayne's English Authors' series; good chapter on 'The Dramatist'.

Ginger, John, *The Notable Man* (Hamish Hamilton, 1977). Biographical and critical study; chapter 12 is mainly on *She Stoops to Conquer*.

Harris, Bernard, 'Goldsmith in the Theatre', in *The Art of Oliver Goldsmith*, ed. Andrew Swarbrick (Barnes and Noble, 1984), pp. 144–67.

Hawthorn, Jeremy, *Multiple Personality and the Disintegration of Literary Character* (Arnold, 1983). Chapter 3 on *She Stoops to Conquer*; interesting.

McCarthy, B. Eugene, 'The Theme of Liberty in *She Stoops to Conquer*', *University of Windsor Review*, vol. 7 (1971) 1–8.

Mikhail, E. H., ed., *Goldsmith: Interviews and Recollections* (Macmillan, 1993). Useful collection of biographical sources.

Nelson, T. G. A., 'Stooping to Conquer in Goldsmith, Haywood and Wycherley', *Essays in Criticism*, vol. 46 (1996) 319–39. Marlow's malady.

Quintana, Ricardo, *Oliver Goldsmith: A Georgian Study* (Macmillan, 1967). Critical study of Goldsmith's work as a whole.

Rousseau, G. S., ed., *Oliver Goldsmith: The Critical Heritage* (Routledge & Kegan Paul, 1974). Includes early reviews of *She Stoops to Conquer*.

Sampson, H. Grant, 'Comic Patterns in Goldsmith's Plays', *English Studies in Canada*, vol. 10 (1984) 36–49.

Smith, John Harrington, 'Tony Lumpkin and the Country Booby Type in Antecedent English Comedy', *PMLA*, vol. 58 (1944) 1038–49.

Styan, J. L., 'Goldsmith's Comic Skills', *Costerus*, vol. 9 (1973) 195–217. The plays in the theatre.

Swarbrick, Andrew, *Goldsmith's She Stoops to Conquer* (Penguin, 1986). 'Passnotes' series; intended for school examination candidates.

Tucker, Herbert W., 'Goldsmith's Comic Monster', *Studies in English Literature*, vol. 19 (1979) 493–9. Appreciation of Lumpkin.

Wardle, R. M., *Oliver Goldsmith* (Lawrence, Kansas University Press; London, Constable, 1957). Reliable and readable biography.

Worth, Katharine, *Sheridan and Goldsmith* (Macmillan, 1992). Valuable throughout; chapter 5 on *She Stoops to Conquer*.

Reference

Woods, Samuel H., Jr., *Oliver Goldsmith: A Reference Guide* (G. K. Hall, 1982). Annotated chronological list of writings about Goldsmith.

ABBREVIATIONS

Bell	*She Stoops to Conquer* (John Bell, 1791). 'British Library' series.
Biographical Dictionary	Edward A. Langhans and others, eds., *A Biographical Dictionary of Stage Personnel in London, 1660–1800* (16 vols., Southern Illinois University Press, 1973–93).
Boswell	James Boswell, *Life of Johnson* (Oxford, 1957). Page references to this 'Oxford Standard Authors' edition.
Cooke	*Comedy of She Stoops to Conquer* (C. Cooke, [1817]). 'Cooke's Edition'.
Davis	Tom Davis, ed., *She Stoops to Conquer* (New Mermaid, 1979).
ed.	(in textual notes) this edition; (elsewhere) either 'edited by' or 'edition'.
Friedman	Arthur Friedman, ed., *She Stoops to Conquer*, in *Works*, vol. V.
Inchbald	*She Stoops to Conquer with Remarks by Mrs Inchbald* (Longman and others, [1806]).
Johnson	Samuel Johnson, *Dictionary* (1755).
L	Larpent manuscript of *She Stoops to Conquer*, Henry Huntington Library.
Letters	Katharine C. Balderston, ed., *The Collected Letters of Oliver Goldsmith* (Cambridge, 1928).
OED	*Oxford English Dictionary* (2nd ed., 1989).
Partridge	Eric Partridge, *A Dictionary of Historical Slang* (Penguin, 1972).
Poems	Roger Lonsdale, ed., *The Poems of Gray, Collins and Goldsmith* (Longman, 1992).
Q	The second reprint of the first quarto of *She Stoops to Conquer* (Newbery, 1773).
s.d.	stage direction
s.p.	speech prefix, i.e. the name of a character prefixed to a speech
Shakespeare	References to *The Complete Works*, ed. Stanley Wells and Gary Taylor (Oxford, 1986).
The London Stage	George Winchester Stone, Jr., ed., *The London Stage, Part IV, 1747–1776* (3 vols., Southern Illinois University Press, 1962).
Works	*Collected Works of Oliver Goldsmith*, ed. Arthur Friedman (5 vols., Oxford, 1966).

SheStoopstoConquer:

O R,

The Miſtakes of a Night.

A

C O M E D Y.

AS IT IS ACTED AT THE

T H E A T R E - R O Y A L

I N

C O V E N T - G A R D E N.

WRITTEN BY

Doctor G O L D S M I T H.

L O N D O N:

Printed for F. NEWBERY, in St. Paul's Church-Yard,

M DCC LXXIII.

12.0.519

1

Title Page

She Stoops to Conquer Q (The Novel L) The Q title was substituted just before the first performance, and Miss Hardcastle's speech about preserving 'the character in which I conquered' (L) was changed to 'the character in which I stooped to conquer' (Q; IV.i.244–5). Goldsmith may have remembered the concluding couplet in Act III of Dryden's *Amphitryon*, 'The offending lover, when he lowest lies, / Submits, to conquer, and but kneels, to rise'. In one of Goldsmith's rejected epilogues for the play are the lines 'Our author ... Still stoops among the low to copy nature' (*Poems*, p. 729), which suggest an analogy between the heroine and the author himself.

DEDICATION

To SAMUEL JOHNSON, L.L.D.

Dear Sir,

By inscribing this slight performance to you, I do not mean so much to compliment you as myself. It may do me some honour to inform the public, that I have lived many years in intimacy with you. It may serve the interests of mankind also to inform them, that the greatest wit may be found in a char-   5
acter, without impairing the most unaffected piety.

I have, particularly, reason to thank you for your partiality to this performance. The undertaking a comedy, not merely sentimental, was very dangerous; and Mr Colman, who saw this piece in its various stages, always thought it so. However   10
I ventured to trust it to the public; and though it was necess-arily delayed till late in the season, I have every reason to be grateful.

I am, Dear Sir,
Your most sincere friend,
And admirer,
OLIVER GOLDSMITH

7–11 As 'a comedy, not merely sentimental' the play opposed 'the vitiated taste of the times' (*Morning Chronicle*, 16 March 1773). Hence George Colman, the Manager of Covent Garden, rejected it at first but, said Johnson, 'was prevailed on at last by much solicitation, nay, a kind of force, to bring it on' (Boswell, 25 April 1778). Johnson, Sir Joshua Reynolds, Edmund Burke and other literary men attended the first night, but their support was no longer needed; the play was a great success. Goldsmith here generously refrains from saying what he really thought of Colman.

11–13 There were twelve performances between 15 March and the end of the season on 31 May, including three benefit nights which realised just over £500 for the author (*The London Stage*).

DRAMATIS PERSONAE

MEN

SIR CHARLES MARLOW	*Mr Gardner*
Young MARLOW (*his son*)	*Mr Lewes*
HARDCASTLE	*Mr Shuter*
HASTINGS	*Mr Dubellamy*
TONY LUMPKIN	*Mr Quick*
DIGGORY	*Mr Saunders*

WOMEN

MRS HARDCASTLE	*Mrs Green*
MISS HARDCASTLE	*Mrs Bulkely*
MISS NEVILLE	*Mrs Kniveton*
MAID	*Miss Willems*

LANDLORD, SERVANTS, &C. &C.

Dramatis Personae This cast list is placed after the prologue in Q.

MARLOW: an undistinguished name compared with Hastings. Young Marlow is called Charles after his father (II.i.64). Maybe Goldsmith knew that Christopher Marlowe the playwright was murdered at an inn.

HARDCASTLE: perhaps meant to recall the old saying, 'An Englishman's house is his castle'. His Christian name is Richard (V.i.17).

HASTINGS: family name of the Earls of Huntingdon; Warren Hastings became Governor of Bengal in 1772. Perhaps Hardcastle thinks there is some connexion (II.i.210–12). His Christian name is George (II.i.74).

TONY LUMPKIN: a Captain Anthony Lumpkin, who died in 1780, is commemorated in the church at Leverington, Cambridgeshire. Goldsmith may have known his family, but probably the name was chosen for its rhyme with 'bumpkin' and its connotations of size, awkwardness and earthiness.

DIGGORY: a Christian name associated with the West Country.

MRS HARDCASTLE: probably born a Blenkinsop (II.i.563 and note). Her Christian name is Dorothy (I.i.22), which was pronounced 'Dorotty'.

MISS HARDCASTLE: her Christian name is Katherine, characteristically shortened by her father to Kate, the old-fashioned form; not to Kitty, the more usual eighteenth-century form. The name has connotations of high-spiritedness, if we think of the heroine of *The Taming of the Shrew*.

MISS NEVILLE: an aristocratic name, like Hastings. Her Christian name is Constance (II.i.310), and she knows its significance (IV.i.424–6).

MAID: Miss Hardcastle's, named Pimple (III.i.231).

LANDLORD: nicknamed Stingo after his ale (I.ii.60).

SERVANTS: Hardcastle's, 'three or four' (s.d., II.i.0), of whom Diggory (II.i.9), Roger (II.i.10) and Thomas (IV.i.357) are named; Marlow's and Hastings's, of whom several are mentioned, but only Jeremy (IV.i.116) is named.

&c. &c. 'Several shabby fellows' (s.d., I.ii.0), four to be precise, Tony's drinking companions. The first is presumably Tom Twist (I.i.76), the second Jack Slang the horse-doctor (I.i.75, ii.48), the third presumably little Aminadab (I.i.75–6, ii.41–5) and the fourth Dick Muggins the exciseman (I.i.74, ii.41). See note to I.i.74–6.

Players

Gardner, William (d. 1790), a journeyman actor at Covent Garden, whose first recorded appearance on the London stage was in 1761.

Lewes, Charles Lee (1740–1803), a distinguished comedian, whose roles had included Cloten in *Cymbeline*, Fabian in *Twelfth Night*, Gratiano in *The Merchant of Venice* and Lofty in *The Good-Natured Man*. When 'Gentleman' Smith turned down the part of Marlow, Lewes played it very successfully, and a delighted Goldsmith wrote a special epilogue for his benefit in May 1773. Later roles included Lucio in *Measure for Measure*. He was the grandfather of G. H. Lewes the partner of George Eliot.

Shuter, Edward (1728?–76), a great comedian, whose earliest successes were as Master Stephen in *Every Man in his Humour*, and Scrub in *The Beaux' Stratagem*. His roles had also included Touchstone, Falstaff, Sir John Brute in *The Provoked Wife*, Polonius, Shylock, and Croaker in *The Good-Natured Man*. Later he created the role of Sir Anthony Absolute in *The Rivals*. In real life he was a wit, drunkard, and follower of Whitefield the Methodist preacher.

Dubellamy, Charles Clementine, stage name of John Evans (d. 1793), a handsome man and an excellent singer, but a moderate actor.

Quick, John (1748–1831) had played Postboy in *The Good-Natured Man*. As Tony Lumpkin 'he scored his first great triumph in a role superbly suited to his whimsical and exuberant talent' (*Biographical Dictionary*). He created the role of Bob Acres in *The Rivals*.

Saunders (fl. 1754–73), a bit-part player at Covent Garden. 'By seeing Mr Saunders, Mr Holtom, Mr Thompson, and Mr Bates, appear in two or three dresses, we should have imagined the Covent Garden company was thin, were we not certain of the contrary' (*Morning Chronicle*, 16 March 1773). A playbill for the first performance (Huntington Library theatre collection) mentions Thompson, Davis, Stoppelaer and Bates as taking small parts. Probably Saunders doubled as Diggory and the Landlord, and the others as servants and Tony's drinking companions.

Green, Mrs Henry, *née* Jane Hippisley (1719–91), an experienced actress. Early corpulence forced her to play hoydens (Cherry in *The Beaux' Stratagem*), conspiratorial chambermaids (Maria in *Twelfth Night*) and eccentrics (Lady Froth in *The Double-Dealer*). She created the roles of Garnet in *The Good-Natured Man* and Mrs Malaprop in *The Rivals*.

Bulkely, Mrs George, *née* Mary Wilford (1748–92), a beautiful woman with many lovers, and a talented actress in comedy. She played most Shakespearean comic heroines, Mrs Frail in *Love for Love*, and Mrs Sullen in *The Beaux' Stratagem*. She created the roles of Miss Richland in *The Good-Natured Man* and Julia in *The Rivals*.

Kniveton, Mrs Thomas, *née* Margaretta Priscilla Ward (d. 1793), an attractive woman and a good actress. She made her début as Juliet at Covent Garden in 1764. Other roles there had included Cherry in *The Beaux' Stratagem* and Margery in *The Country Wife*.

Willems, Miss, probably a daughter of Mrs Willems (fl. 1767–81), a dancer and singer, at Covent Garden during the 1772–3 season.

PROLOGUE

By DAVID GARRICK, Esq.

Enter Mr WOODWARD,
dressed in black, and holding a handkerchief to his eyes

Excuse me, sirs, I pray – I can't yet speak –
I'm crying now – and have been all the week!
'Tis not alone this mourning suit, good masters;
I've that within – for which there are no plasters!
Pray would you know the reason why I'm crying?   5
The comic muse, long sick, is now a-dying!
And if she goes, my tears will never stop;
For as a player, I can't squeeze out one drop:
I am undone, that's all – shall lose my bread –
I'd rather, but that's nothing – lose my head.   10
When the sweet maid is laid upon the bier,
Shuter and I shall be chief mourners here.
To *her* a mawkish drab of spurious breed,
Who deals in *sentimentals,* will succeed!
Poor *Ned* and *I* are dead to all intents,   15
We can as soon speak *Greek* as *sentiments!*
Both nervous grown, to keep our spirits up,
We now and then take down a hearty cup.
What shall we do? – If Comedy forsake us!

0.2 GARRICK Manager of the rival theatre at Drury Lane. He may have written this
   prologue because Goldsmith supported his election to 'The Club' founded by
   Reynolds, Johnson, Goldsmith and others.
0.3 s.d. WOODWARD Henry Woodward (1714–77), a leading comedian at Covent
   Garden, said to have turned down the role of Tony Lumpkin, for which he was
   certainly too old.
3–4 *'Tis not ... within* Alluding to *Hamlet,* I.ii.77, 85: ''Tis not alone my inky
   cloak, good mother ... I have that within which passeth show'.
11, 33 *maid* 'the comic muse' (l. 6)
12–18 Edward Shuter, who played Hardcastle, sometimes took the stage drunk. See
   note on him opposite.
14, 16 *sentimentals, sentiments* i.e. sentimental comedy and its usual sententious
   moralising, parodied in ll. 25–30.

They'll turn us out, and no one else will take us.   20
But why can't I be moral? – Let me try –
My heart thus pressing – fixed my face and eye –
With a sententious look, that nothing means,
(Faces are blocks, in sentimental scenes)
Thus I begin – *All is not gold that glitters,*   25
Pleasure seems sweet, but proves a glass of bitters.
When ignorance enters, folly is at hand;
Learning is better far than house and land:
Let not your virtue trip, who trips may stumble,
And virtue is not virtue, if she tumble.   30
   I give it up – morals won't do for me;
To make you laugh I must play tragedy.
One hope remains – hearing the maid was ill,
A *doctor* comes this night to show his skill.
To cheer her heart, and give your muscles motion,   35
He in *five draughts* prepared, presents a potion:
A kind of magic charm – for be assured,
If you will *swallow* it, the maid is cured:
But desperate the Doctor, and her case is,
If you reject the dose, and make wry faces!   40
This truth he boasts, will boast it while he lives,
No *poisonous drugs* are mixed in what he gives;
Should he succeed, you'll give him his degree;
If not, within he will receive no fee!
The college *you*, must his pretensions back,   45
Pronounce him *regular*, or dub him *quack*.

20 Quoting Buckingham, *The Rehearsal*, II.iv.62–3: 'they'll turn us out, and nobody else will take us'.

24 *blocks* featureless wooden heads, used as wig-stands

34, 43 *doctor, degree* The dramatist himself was known as Dr Goldsmith, and had practised medicine, though whether he had a degree was uncertain.

36 *five draughts* the five Acts of the play

45 *college you* the audience, acting as the College of Physicians

46 *regular* qualified
   quack charlatan, especially in medicine

SHE STOOPS TO CONQUER:

or,

THE MISTAKES OF A NIGHT

Act I, Scene i

Scene. A chamber in an old-fashioned house

Enter MRS HARDCASTLE *and* MR HARDCASTLE

MRS HARDCASTLE

I vow, Mr Hardcastle, you're very particular. Is there a
creature in the whole country, but ourselves, that does not
take a trip to town now and then, to rub off the rust a little?
There's the two Miss Hoggs, and our neighbour, Mrs
Grigsby, go to take a month's polishing every winter.   5

HARDCASTLE

Ay, and bring back vanity and affectation to last them the
whole year. I wonder why London cannot keep its own
fools at home. In my time, the follies of the town crept
slowly among us, but now they travel faster than a stage-
coach. Its fopperies come down, not only as inside passen-   10
gers, but in the very basket.

MRS HARDCASTLE

Ay, *your* times were fine times, indeed; you have been
telling us of *them* for many a long year. Here we live in an
old rambling mansion, that looks for all the world like an
inn, but that we never see company. Our best visitors are   15
old Mrs Oddfish, the curate's wife, and little Cripplegate,
the lame dancing-master: and all our entertainment your

---

2 *country* (here) neighbourhood, county
4–5 *Hoggs ... Grigsby* In this play most invented surnames and place names are
   significant; Goldsmith knew the saying 'as merry as a grig' (reveller) – *Works*,
   vol. III p. 137.
11 *basket* outside back seat or baggage rack
14 *rambling* L (rumbling Q), irregularly planned. Mrs Hardcastle is saying the
   house 'looks' like an inn.

old stories of Prince Eugene and the Duke of Marlborough.
I hate such old-fashioned trumpery.

HARDCASTLE

And I love it. I love everything that's old: old friends, old   20
times, old manners, old books, old wine; and I believe,
Dorothy, (*taking her hand*) you'll own I have been pretty
fond of an old wife.

MRS HARDCASTLE

Lord, Mr Hardcastle, you're for ever at your 'Dorothys'
and your 'old wifes'. You may be a Darby, but I'll be no   25
Joan, I promise you. I'm not so old as you'd make me, by
more than one good year. Add twenty to twenty, and make
money of that.

HARDCASTLE

Let me see; twenty added to twenty, makes just fifty and
seven.   30

MRS HARDCASTLE

It's false, Mr Hardcastle: I was but twenty when I was
brought to bed of Tony, that I had by Mr Lumpkin, my first
husband; and he's not come to years of discretion yet.

HARDCASTLE

Nor ever will, I dare answer for him. Ay, you have taught
him finely.   35

MRS HARDCASTLE

No matter, Tony Lumpkin has a good fortune. My son is
not to live by his learning. I don't think a boy wants much
learning to spend fifteen hundred a year.

HARDCASTLE

Learning, quotha! A mere composition of tricks and mischief.   40

MRS HARDCASTLE

Humour, my dear: nothing but humour. Come, Mr Hardcastle, you must allow the boy a little humour.

---

18 *Prince Eugene ... Marlborough* The leaders of the Austrian and British armies in
   the War of the Spanish Succession (1701–14).

19 *trumpery* nonsense

25–6 *Darby ... Joan* typical elderly affectionate couple

27–8 *make money* make what you can

33 *years of discretion* (legally) age when a person was presumed able to exercise discretion, i.e. fourteen. But Tony is apparently twenty (l. 27 above) and really
   twenty-one, legally of age, though the Hardcastles conceal the fact from him
   (V.iii.134–8).

39 *quotha* quoth she, i.e. 'said she' spoken sarcastically

41 *humour ... humour* Q (spirit ... spirit L); humour retained its old sense of tem-
   perament

HARDCASTLE

I'd sooner allow him a horsepond. If burning the footmen's
shoes, frighting the maids, and worrying the kittens, be
humour, he has it. It was but yesterday he fastened my wig   45
to the back of my chair, and when I went to make a bow, I
popped my bald head in Mrs Frizzle's face.

MRS HARDCASTLE

And am I to blame? The poor boy was always too sickly to
do any good. A school would be his death. When he comes
to be a little stronger, who knows what a year or two's   50
Latin may do for him?

HARDCASTLE

Latin for him! A cat and fiddle. No, no, the ale-house and
the stable are the only schools he'll ever go to.

MRS HARDCASTLE

Well, we must not snub the poor boy now, for I believe we
shan't have him long among us. Anybody that looks in his   55
face may see he's consumptive.

HARDCASTLE

Ay, if growing too fat be one of the symptoms.

MRS HARDCASTLE

He coughs sometimes.

HARDCASTLE

Yes, when his liquor goes the wrong way.

MRS HARDCASTLE

I'm actually afraid of his lungs.   60

HARDCASTLE

And truly so am I; for he sometimes whoops like a speaking-trumpet. – (TONY *hallooing behind the scenes*) – Oh
there he goes! –

Enter TONY, *crossing the stage*

A very consumptive figure, truly.

MRS HARDCASTLE

Tony, where are you going, my charmer? Won't you give   65
papa and I a little of your company, lovey?

TONY

I'm in haste, mother, I cannot stay.

---

43 *horsepond* pond for watering and washing horses, or ducking nuisances
47 *Frizzle* see note to ll. 4–5. above; frizzle meant crisp curly hair
52 *cat and fiddle* unlikely combination (proverbial)
61–2 *speaking-trumpet* megaphone
62 s.d. *hallooing* shouting 'halloo' as if to urge on hounds; *scenes* scenery
63 s.d. *Enter ... stage.* ed. (Q has it after next line). Hardcastle's sarcasm will be
    funnier if Tony has entered.

MRS HARDCASTLE
You shan't venture out this raw evening, my dear: you look
most shockingly.

TONY
I can't stay, I tell you. The Three Pigeons expects me down   70
every moment. There's some fun going forward.

HARDCASTLE
Ay; the ale-house, the old place: I thought so.

MRS HARDCASTLE
A low, paltry set of fellows.

TONY
Not so low neither. There's Dick Muggins the exciseman,
Jack Slang the horse doctor, little Aminadab that grinds the   75
music box, and Tom Twist that spins the pewter platter.

MRS HARDCASTLE
Pray, my dear, disappoint them for one night at least.

TONY
As for disappointing *them*, I should not so much mind; but
I can't abide to disappoint *myself*.

MRS HARDCASTLE (*Detaining him*)
You shan't go.   80

TONY
I will, I tell you.

MRS HARDCASTLE
I say you shan't.

TONY
We'll see which is strongest, you or I.

Exit, hauling her out

HARDCASTLE
Ay, there goes a pair that only spoil each other. But is not
the whole age in a combination to drive sense and discre-   85
tion out of doors? There's my pretty darling Kate; the fashions of the times have almost infected her too. By living a
year or two in town, she is come to be as fond of gauze, and
Paris nets, and French frippery, as the best of them.

---

73 *low* lower-class, vulgar

74–6 Tony ignores the vulgar names and lower-class occupations of his drinking
companions. A muggins is a fool, slang is vulgar language, and Aminadab is presumably a Jew. An exciseman was a collector of taxes on imports, a music box
was a barrel organ, and Tom Twist probably sings to the accompaniment of a
spinning plate: see *Works*, vol. III p. 9.

87–9 L is both clearer and more theatrical.

88 *is come to be* L (is Q)

88–9 *and Paris nets* L (Q omits)

Enter MISS HARDCASTLE

Blessings on my pretty innocence! Dressed out as usual, my   90
Kate. Goodness! What a quantity of superfluous silk hast
thou got about thee, girl! I can never teach the fools of this
age, that the nakedness of the indigent world could be
clothed out of the trimmings of the vain.

MISS HARDCASTLE
You know our agreement, sir. You allow me the morning   95
to receive and pay visits, and to dress in my own manner;
and in the evening, I put on my housewife's dress to please
you.

HARDCASTLE
Well, remember I insist on the terms of our agreement; and
by the bye, I believe I shall have occasion to try your obe-   100
dience this very evening.

MISS HARDCASTLE
I protest, sir, I don't comprehend your meaning.

HARDCASTLE
Then, to be plain with you, Kate, I expect the young gentleman I have chosen to be your husband from town this very
day. I have his father's letter, in which he informs me his   105
son is set out, and that he intends to follow himself shortly
after.

MISS HARDCASTLE
Indeed! I wish I had known something of this before. Bless
me, how shall I behave? It's a thousand to one I shan't like
him; our meeting will be so formal, and so like a thing of   110
business, that I shall find no room for friendship or esteem.

HARDCASTLE
Depend upon it, child, I'll never control your choice; but
Mr Marlow, whom I have pitched upon, is the son of my
old friend, Sir Charles Marlow, of whom you have heard
me talk so often. The young gentleman has been bred a   115
scholar, and is designed for an employment in the service of
his country. I am told he's a man of an excellent understanding.

---

92   *can* L (could Q): he is still trying
93   *the nakedness of* L (Q omits)
93–4   *the nakedness … the vain* Quotation from *The Vicar of Wakefield*, ch. iv,
    derived from William Penn, *Some Fruits of Solitude* (7th edn., 1718, p. 32): 'The
    very Trimmings of the vain world would cloath all the naked one'.
113   *pitched upon* happened to choose

MISS HARDCASTLE
  Is he?

HARDCASTLE
  Very generous.   120

MISS HARDCASTLE
  I believe I shall like him.

HARDCASTLE
  Young and brave.

MISS HARDCASTLE
  I'm sure I shall like him.

HARDCASTLE
  And very handsome.

MISS HARDCASTLE
  My dear Papa, say no more (*kissing his hand*), he's mine, 125
  I'll have him.

HARDCASTLE
  And to crown all, Kate, he's one of the most bashful and
  reserved young fellows in all the world.

MISS HARDCASTLE
  Eh! you have frozen me to death again. That word reserved,
  has undone all the rest of his accomplishments. A reserved 130
  lover, it is said, always makes a suspicious husband.

HARDCASTLE
  On the contrary, modesty seldom resides in a breast that is
  not enriched with nobler virtues. It was the very feature in
  his character that first struck me.

MISS HARDCASTLE
  He must have more striking features to catch me, I promise 135
  you. However, if he be so young, so handsome, and so
  everything you mention, I believe he'll do still. I think I'll
  have him.

HARDCASTLE
  Ay, Kate, but there is still an obstacle. It's more than an
  even wager, he may not have *you*.   140

MISS HARDCASTLE
  My dear Papa, why will you mortify one so? – Well, if he
  refuses, instead of breaking my heart at his indifference, I'll
  only break my glass for its flattery, set my cap to some
  newer fashion, and look out for some less difficult admirer.

HARDCASTLE
  Bravely resolved! In the meantime I'll go prepare the ser- 145
  vants for his reception; as we seldom see company they

---

137 *everything* ed. (every thing L, every thing, as Q). L is unambiguous.

want as much training as a company of recruits, the first
day's muster.   *Exit*
MISS HARDCASTLE
Lud, this news of Papa's, puts me all in a flutter. Young,
handsome; these he put last; but I put them foremost.   150
Sensible, good-natured; I like all that. But then reserved,
and sheepish, that's much against him. Yet can't he be
cured of his timidity, by being taught to be proud of his
wife? Yes, and can't I – But I vow I'm disposing of the husband, before I have secured the lover.   155

                    Enter MISS NEVILLE

I'm glad you're come, Neville my dear. Tell me, Constance,
how do I look this evening? Is there anything whimsical
about me? Is it one of my well-looking days, child? Am I in
face today?
MISS NEVILLE
Perfectly, my dear. Yet now I look again – bless me! – sure   160
no accident has happened among the canary birds or the
gold fishes? Has your brother or the cat been meddling? Or
has the last novel been too moving?
MISS HARDCASTLE
No; nothing of all this. I have been threatened – I can scarce
get it out – I have been threatened with a lover.   165
MISS NEVILLE
And his name –
MISS HARDCASTLE
Is Marlow.
MISS NEVILLE
Indeed!
MISS HARDCASTLE
The son of Sir Charles Marlow.
MISS NEVILLE
As I live, the most intimate friend of Mr Hastings, *my*   170
admirer. They are never asunder. I believe you must have
seen him when we lived in town.
MISS HARDCASTLE
Never.

148 *muster* assembly; Hardcastle was once an army officer
157 *whimsical* odd
158 *child* attendant
158–9 *in face* looking my best
160–5 Images of weeping over pets or novels mockingly anticipate the idea of meet-
    ing a lover.

MISS NEVILLE

He's a very singular character, I assure you. Among women
of reputation and virtue, he is the modestest man alive; but 175
his acquaintance give him a very different character among
creatures of another stamp: you understand me.

MISS HARDCASTLE

An odd character, indeed. I shall never be able to manage
him. What shall I do? Pshaw, think no more of him, but
trust to occurrences for success. But how goes on your own 180
affair my dear? Has my mother been courting you for my
brother Tony, as usual?

MISS NEVILLE

I have just come from one of our agreeable tête-à-têtes. She
has been saying a hundred tender things, and setting off her
pretty monster as the very pink of perfection. 185

MISS HARDCASTLE

And her partiality is such, that she actually thinks him so.
A fortune like yours is no small temptation. Besides, as she
has the sole management of it, I'm not surprised to see her
unwilling to let it go out of the family.

MISS NEVILLE

A fortune like mine, which chiefly consists in jewels, is no 190
such mighty temptation. But at any rate if my dear Hastings
be but constant, I make no doubt to be too hard for her at
last. However, I let her suppose that I am in love with her
son, and she never once dreams that my affections are fixed
upon another. 195

MISS HARDCASTLE

My good brother holds out stoutly. I could almost love him
for hating you so.

MISS NEVILLE

It is a good-natured creature at bottom, and I'm sure would
wish to see me married to anybody but himself. (*A bell
rings*) But my aunt's bell rings for our afternoon's walk 200
round the improvements. *Allons.* Courage is necessary as
our affairs are critical.

---

177 *creatures of another stamp* women of a different kind, such as actresses or prostitutes
179 *Pshaw* (here) exclamation of impatience
184 *setting off* giving a flattering description of
185 *pink* flower, extreme
199–200 s.d. L (Q omits)
201 *improvements* new enclosures, gardens or buildings; presumably, more to Mrs
Hardcastle's taste than to her husband's
Allons Come on (French)

MISS HARDCASTLE
Would it were bedtime and all were well.

Exeunt

[Act I, Scene ii]

Scene. An alehouse room.

Several shabby fellows, with punch and tobacco. TONY
at the head of the table, a little higher than the rest; a
mallet in his hand.

OMNES
Hurrah, hurrah, hurrah, bravo!
FIRST FELLOW
Now, gentlemen, silence for a song. The Squire is going to
knock himself down for a song.
OMNES
Ay, a song, a song!
TONY
Then I'll sing you, gentlemen, a song I made upon this ale-   5
house, the Three Pigeons.

SONG

Let schoolmasters puzzle their brain,
    With grammar, and nonsense, and learning;
Good liquor, I stoutly maintain,
    Gives *genus* a better discerning.   10
Let them brag of their heathenish gods,
    Their Lethes, their Styxes, and Stygians;
Their *quis*, and their *quaes*, and their *quods*,

---

203 *Would ... well* Alluding to Falstaff's speech before the Battle of Shrewsbury, 'I
    would 'twere bed-time, Hal, and all well' (*Henry IV Part I*, V.i.126).

  0 s.d. 2 *punch* wine or spirits mixed with hot water or milk, sweetened with such
    ingredients as sugar, spice and lemon

  1 s.p. OMNES All (Latin)

  3 *knock ... song* sell himself cheaply; auctioneering expression, prompted by
    Tony's use of his mallet

  7–14 Schoolmasters taught Latin mythology and grammar. *Lethe* and *Styx* were
    rivers in the underworld; *Stygians* spirits living by the Styx, a Lumpkinism. As
    every schoolboy knew, *qui*, *quae* and *quod* are the nominative forms of the rela-
    tive pronoun.

 10 *genus* Tony's version of 'genius'

They're all but a parcel of pigeons.
     Toroddle, toroddle, toroll.   15
When Methodist preachers come down,
 A-preaching that drinking is sinful,
I'll wager the rascals a crown,
 They always preach best with a skinful.
But when you come down with your pence,   20
 For a slice of their scurvy religion,
I'll leave it to all men of sense,
 But you my good friend are the pigeon.
     Toroddle, toroddle, toroll.
Then come, put the jorum about,   25
 And let us be merry and clever,
Our hearts and our liquors are stout,
 Here's the Three Jolly Pigeons for ever.
Let some cry up woodcock or hare,
 Your bustards, your ducks, and your widgeons; 30
But of all the birds in the air,
 Here's a health to the Three Jolly Pigeons.
     Toroddle, toroddle, toroll.

OMNES
Bravo, bravo.
FIRST FELLOW
The Squire has got spunk in him.   35
SECOND FELLOW
I loves to hear him sing, bekeays he never gives us nothing
that's *low*.
THIRD FELLOW
Oh damn anything that's *low*, I cannot bear it.

---

14 *parcel of pigeons* lot of fools
16 *Methodist preachers* followers of John Wesley and George Whitefield, who
 toured the country preaching repentance for sin, including drunkenness
19 *skinful* as much as they can drink
21 *scurvy* worthless
25 *jorum* large drinking vessel
35 *spunk* spirit
36 *loves, bekeays* Here and elsewhere non-standard grammar and spelling indicate
 dialect speech.
37 *low* vulgar (as at I.i.73). A puppet-master, a clerk and an exciseman, in a dis-
 cussion at an inn, make similar objections to 'low' comedy in Fielding's *Tom
 Jones* (1749) Book XII ch. v. Goldsmith's *Good-Natured Man* had been criti-
 cised for the bailiffs' scene; see Introduction, p. xiv

FOURTH FELLOW

The genteel thing is the genteel thing at any time. If so be
that a gentleman bes in a concatination ackoardingly.   40

THIRD FELLOW

I like the maxum of it, Master Muggins. What though I am
obligated to dance a bear; a man may be a gentleman for all
that. May this be my poison if my bear ever dances but to
the very genteelest of tunes. 'Water Parted', or the minuet
in *Ariadne*.   45

SECOND FELLOW

What a pity it is the Squire is not come to his own. It would
be well for all the publicans within ten miles round of him.

TONY

Ecod and so it would Master Slang. I'd then show what it
was to keep choice of company.

SECOND FELLOW

Oh he takes after his own father for that. To be sure old   50
Squire Lumpkin was the finest gentleman I ever set my eyes
on. For winding the straight horn, or beating a thicket for
a hare, or a wench, he never had his fellow. It was a saying
in the place, that he kept the best horses, dogs and girls in
the whole county.   55

TONY

Ecod, and when I'm of age I'll be no bastard I promise you.
I have been thinking of Bet Bouncer and the miller's grey
mare to begin with. But come, my boys, drink about and be
merry, for you pay no reckoning.

Enter LANDLORD

Well Stingo, what's the matter?   60

LANDLORD

There be two gentlemen in a post-chaise at the door. They

---

40 *bes in a concatination ackoardingly* is determined to think so; an attempt at
'high' style

concatination ackoardingly L (concatenation accordingly Q)

41 *maxum* maxim, sententious saying

42–3 *a man ... all that* Anticipates Burns, 'A man's a man for a' that' (Song, 'Is
there, for honest poverty', 1790).

44 '*Water Parted*' aria from Arne's opera *Artaxerxes* (1762)

45 *Ariadne* Handel's opera *Arianna* (1734)

46 *come to his own* come into his inheritance, by coming of age; see note to I.i.33

56 *bastard* Q (Changeling L)

60 *Stingo* The landlord's nickname is a slang term for strong beer.

61 *post-chaise* hired carriage

have lost their way upo' the forest; and they are talking
something about Mr Hardcastle.

TONY
As sure as can be one of them must be the gentleman that's
coming down to court my sister. Do they seem to be   65
Londoners?

LANDLORD
I believe they may. They look woundily like Frenchmen.

TONY
Then desire them to step this way, and I'll set them right in
a twinkling.

Exit LANDLORD

Gentlemen, as they mayn't be good enough company for   70
you, step down for a moment, and I'll be with you in the
squeezing of a lemon.

Exeunt mob

Father-in-law has been calling me whelp, and hound, this
half year. Now if I pleased, I could be so revenged upon the
old grumbletonian. But then I'm afraid – afraid of what? I   75
shall soon be worth fifteen hundred a year, and let him
frighten me out of *that* if he can.

Enter LANDLORD, *conducting* MARLOW *and* HASTINGS

MARLOW
What a tedious uncomfortable day have we had of it! We
were told it was but forty miles across the country, and we
have come above threescore.   80

HASTINGS
And all, Marlow, from that unaccountable reserve of yours,
that would not let us enquire more frequently on the way.

MARLOW
I own, Hastings, I am unwilling to lay myself under an obligation to everyone I meet; and often stand the chance of an
unmannerly answer.   85

HASTINGS
At present, however, we are not likely to receive any
answer.

---

62 *upo'* Q (upon L)
67 *woundily* dreadfully
73 *Father-in-law* Step-father
75 *grumbletonian* Q (Grumbletonian L): professional grumbler. In the reign of
    William and Mary the Court party had nicknamed the Country party the
    Grumbletonians.

TONY

No offence, gentlemen. But I'm told you have been enquir-
ing for one Mr Hardcastle, in these parts. Do you know
what part of the country you are in?   90

HASTINGS

Not in the least, sir, but should thank you for information.

TONY

Nor the way you came?

HASTINGS

No, sir; but if you can inform us –

TONY

Why, gentlemen, if you know neither the road you are
going, nor where you are, nor the road you came, the first   95
thing I have to inform you is, that – you have lost your way.

MARLOW

We wanted no ghost to tell us that.

TONY

Pray, gentlemen, may I be so bold as to ask the place from
whence you came?

MARLOW

That's not necessary towards directing us where we are to go.   100

TONY

No offence; but question for question is all fair, you know.
Pray, gentlemen, is not this same Hardcastle a cross-
grained, old-fashioned, whimsical fellow, with an ugly face,
a daughter, and a pretty son?

HASTINGS

We have not seen the gentleman, but he has the family you   105
mention.

TONY

The daughter, a tall, trapesing, trolloping, talkative may-

---

89 *these* L (those Q)

97 *wanted no ghost* Q (did not want any body L). Alluding to Horatio's reply to an
    uninformative speech by Hamlet: 'There needs no ghost, my lord, come from the
    grave, / To tell us this' (*Hamlet* I.v.128–9). Perhaps suggested by Tony's desire
    for revenge (l. 74 above).

102–3 *cross-grained* perverse

107 *tall* Miss Hardcastle may seem 'tall' to Marlow at first (V.iii.81) but she seems
    'little' later (III.i.335, IV.i.30, 43, V.iii.152).
    trapesing walking about aimlessly, gadding about
    trolloping ungainly, slovenly

pole – the son, a pretty, well-bred, agreeable youth, that
everybody is fond of.

MARLOW

Our information differs in this. The daughter is said to be   110
well-bred and beautiful; the son, an awkward booby,
reared up and spoiled at his mother's apron-string.

TONY

He-he-hem! – Then, gentlemen, all I have to tell you is, that
you won't reach Mr Hardcastle's house this night, I believe.

HASTINGS

Unfortunate!   115

TONY

It's a damned long, dark, boggy, dirty, dangerous way.
Stingo, tell the gentlemen the way to Mr Hardcastle's;
(*winking upon the* LANDLORD) Mr Hardcastle's, of
Quagmire Marsh, you understand me.

LANDLORD

Master Hardcastle's! Lack-a-daisy, my masters, you're   120
come a deadly deal wrong! When you came to the bottom
of the hill, you should have crossed down Squash Lane.

MARLOW

Cross down Squash Lane!

LANDLORD

Then you were to keep straight forward, till you came to
four roads.   125

MARLOW

Come to where four roads meet!

TONY

Ay; but you must be sure to take only one of them.

MARLOW

Oh sir, you're facetious.

107–8 *maypole* i.e. tall, thin and painted; term applied abusively by Hermia to
     Helena (*A Midsummer Night's Dream*, III.ii.297)
109 *fond* Q (so fond L)
111 *booby* 'a dull, heavy, stupid fellow' (Johnson)
120 *Lack-a-daisy* L (Lock-a daisy Q), alack the day; vague expression of surprise
122 *Squash* probably signifies splashy rather than narrow; suggested by Quagmire
     Marsh (l. 119 above)
123, 126, 136 L adds the stage-directions *Noting it down*, *Still noting* and *Who had
     been noting*. They are not in Q, Bell, Inchbald or Cooke, so this stage business
     was probably found awkward and not used.

TONY

Then keeping to the right, you are to go sideways till you
come upon Crackskull Common: there you must look   130
sharp for the track of the wheel, and go forward, till you
come to farmer Murrain's barn. Coming to the farmer's
barn, you are to turn to the right, and then to the left,
and then to the right about again, till you find out the old
mill –   135

MARLOW

Zounds, man! we could as soon find out the longitude!

HASTINGS

What's to be done, Marlow?

MARLOW

This house promises but a poor reception; though perhaps
the landlord can accommodate us.

LANDLORD

Alack, master, we have but one spare bed in the whole   140
house.

TONY

And to my knowledge, that's taken up by three lodgers
already. (*After a pause, in which the rest seem disconcerted*)
I have hit it. Don't you think, Stingo, our landlady could
accommodate the gentlemen by the fire-side, with – three   145
chairs and a bolster?

HASTINGS

I hate sleeping by the fire-side.

MARLOW

And I detest your three chairs and a bolster.

TONY

You do, do you? – Then let me see. – What if you go on a
mile further, to the Buck's Head; the old Buck's Head on   150
the hill, one of the best inns in the whole county?

HASTINGS

O ho! so we have escaped an adventure for this night, however.

LANDLORD (*Apart to* TONY)

Sure, you ben't sending them to your father's as an inn, be
you?   155

129–35 Places reminiscent of the fashionable 'Gothic' novels and plays. *Crackskull
Common* is crossed by a dangerous cart track, and may be associated with highwaymen; see V.ii.67–70. *Murrain* suggests plague and death.

136 *longitude* A prize of £20,000 had been offered in 1713 for an exact means of cal-
culating longitude at sea. It was claimed by John Harrison some three months
after the first performance of this play.

TONY

Mum, you fool you. Let *them* find that out. (*To them*) You
have only to keep on straight forward, till you come to a
large old house by the road side. You'll see a pair of large
horns over the door. That's the sign. Drive up the yard, and
call stoutly about you.   160

HASTINGS

Sir, we are obliged to you. The servants can't miss the way?

TONY

No, no. But I must tell you though, the landlord is rich, and
going to leave off business; so he wants to be thought a
gentleman, saving your presence, he! he! he! He'll be for
giving you his company, and, ecod, if you mind him, he'll   165
persuade you that his mother was an alderman, and his
aunt a Justice of Peace.

LANDLORD

A troublesome old blade to be sure; but a' keeps as good
wines and beds as any in the whole county.

MARLOW

Well, if he supplies us with these, we shall want no further   170
connexion. We are to turn to the right, did you say?

TONY

No, no; straight forward. I'll just step myself, and show you
a piece of the way. (*To* LANDLORD) Mum.

LANDLORD

Ah, bless your heart, for a sweet, pleasant – damned mischievous son of a whore.   175

Exeunt

Act II

Scene. An old-fashioned house

Enter HARDCASTLE, *followed by three or four*
awkward SERVANTS

---

162   *must* L (Q omits). L is more emphatically confidential.
164   *saving your presence* without offence to you gentlemen here
168   *old blade* old soldier, lively old fellow
     a' he (dialect form)
169   *county* L (country Q). The landlord echoes Tony (l. 151 above).
171   *connexion* personal relationship

HARDCASTLE

Well, I hope you're perfect in the table exercise I have been
teaching you these three days. You all know your posts and
your places, and can show that you have been used to good
company, without ever stirring from home.

SERVANTS

Ay, ay.   5

HARDCASTLE

When company comes, you are not to pop out and stare,
and then run in again, like frighted rabbits in a warren.

SERVANTS

No, no.

HARDCASTLE

You, Diggory, whom I have taken from the barn, are to
make a show at the side-table; and you, Roger, whom I   10
have advanced from the plough, are to place yourself
behind *my* chair. But you're not to stand so, with your
hands in your pockets. Take your hands from your pockets,
Roger; and from your head, you blockhead you. See how
Diggory carries his hands. They're a little too stiff, indeed,   15
but that's no great matter.

DIGGORY

Ay, mind how I hold them. I learned to hold my hands this
aways, when I was upon drill for the militia. And so being
upon drill –

HARDCASTLE

You must not be so talkative, Diggory. You must be all   20
attention to the guests. You must hear us talk, and not
think of talking; you must see us drink, and not think of
drinking; you must see us eat, and not think of eating.

DIGGORY

By the laws, your worship, that's parfectly unpossible.
Whenever Diggory sees yeating going forward, ecod, he's   25
always wishing for a mouthful himself.

HARDCASTLE

Blockhead! Is not a bellyful in the kitchen as good as a bellyful in the parlour? Stay your stomach with that reflection.

DIGGORY

Ecod, I thank your worship, I'll make a shift to stay my
stomach with a slice of cold beef in the pantry.   30

---

11 *advanced from the plough* like Cincinnatus, 'taken from the plough'
   (Goldsmith's *Roman History*) to the supreme command of the Roman army
18 *aways* L (way Q). Here and elsewhere the servants use dialect.
   militia the auxiliary force, not the regular army; the home guard

HARDCASTLE

Diggory, you are too talkative. Then if I happen to say a
good thing, or tell a good story at table, you must not all
burst out a-laughing, as if you made part of the company.

DIGGORY

Then ecod your worship must not tell the story of ould
Grouse in the gun-room: I can't help laughing at that – he!   35
he! he! – for the soul of me. We have laughed at that these
twenty years – ha! ha! ha!

HARDCASTLE

Ha! ha! ha! The story is a good one. Well, honest Diggory,
you may laugh at that – but still remember to be attentive.
Suppose one of the company should call for a glass of wine,   40
how will you behave? A glass of wine, sir, if you please –
(*To* DIGGORY) Eh, why don't you move?

DIGGORY

Ecod, your worship, I never have courage till I see the eat-
ables and drinkables brought upo' the table, and then I'm
as bauld as a lion.   45

HARDCASTLE

What, will nobody move?

FIRST SERVANT

I'm not to leave this pleace.

SECOND SERVANT

I'm sure it's no pleace of mine.

THIRD SERVANT

Nor mine, for sartain.

DIGGORY

Wauns, and I'm sure it canna be mine.   50

HARDCASTLE

You numbskulls! and so while, like your betters, you are
quarrelling for places, the guests must be starved. Oh you
dunces! I find I must begin all over again. – But don't I hear
a coach drive into the yard? To your posts, you blockheads.
I'll go in the meantime and give my old friend's son a hearty   55
reception at the gate.

Exit HARDCASTLE

---

35 *Grouse* probably a dog
45 *bauld* Q (bold L): bold (dialect)
50 *Wauns* wounds, i.e. God's wounds, a mild oath
52 *places* the servants' domestic positions and their betters' government appoint-
    ments

DIGGORY
By the elevens, my pleace is gone quite out of my head.

ROGER
I know that my pleace is to be everywhere.

FIRST SERVANT
Where the devil is mine?

SECOND SERVANT
My pleace is to be nowhere at all; and so I's go about my   60
business.

Exeunt SERVANTS, *running about as if frighted, different ways*

Enter SERVANT *with candles, showing in* MARLOW *and*
HASTINGS

SERVANT
Welcome, gentlemen, very welcome. This way.

HASTINGS
After the disappointments of the day, welcome once more,
Charles, to the comforts of a clean room and a good fire.
Upon my word, a very well-looking house; antique, but   65
creditable.

MARLOW
The usual fate of a large mansion. Having first ruined the
master by good housekeeping, it at last comes to levy con-
tributions as an inn.

HASTINGS
As you say, we passengers are to be taxed to pay all these   70
fineries. I have often seen a good sideboard, or a marble
chimneypiece, though not actually put in the bill, inflame a
reckoning confoundedly.

MARLOW
Travellers, George, must pay in all places. The only difference is, that in good inns, you pay dearly for luxuries; in   75
bad inns, you are fleeced and starved.

HASTINGS
You have lived pretty much among them. In truth, I have
been often surprised, that you who have seen so much of
the world, with your natural good sense, and your many

---

57 *elevens* (probably) heavens
68 *good housekeeping* keeping a good house, hospitality
70-1 *pay all these fineries* Q, Bell, Inchbald, Cooke (support all this finery L) i.e.
    pay for them (*OED* 12a)
72-3 *inflame a reckoning* increase a bill. In Shakespeare and Fletcher's *Two Noble
    Kinsmen*, III.v.129-32, an innkeeper is said to 'inflame the reck'ning' for
    travellers, 'to their cost'.

opportunities, could never yet acquire a requisite share of   80
assurance.

MARLOW

The Englishman's malady. But tell me, George, where could
I have learned that assurance you talk of? My life has been
chiefly spent in a college, or an inn, in seclusion from that
lovely part of the creation that chiefly teach men confi-   85
dence. I don't know that I was ever familiarly acquainted
with a single modest woman – except my mother. – But
among females of another class you know –

HASTINGS

Ay, among them you are impudent enough of all conscience.   90

MARLOW

They are of *us* you know.

HASTINGS

But in the company of women of reputation I never saw
such an idiot, such a trembler; you look for all the world as
if you wanted an opportunity of stealing out of the room.

MARLOW

Why man that's because I *do* want to steal out of the room.   95
Faith, I have often formed a resolution to break the ice, and
rattle away at any rate. But I don't know how, a single
glance from a pair of fine eyes has totally overset my resolution. An impudent fellow may counterfeit modesty, but I'll
be hanged if a modest man can ever counterfeit impudence.   100

HASTINGS

If you could but say half the fine things to them that I have
heard you lavish upon the barmaid of an inn, or even a college bedmaker –

MARLOW

Why, George, I can't say fine things to them. They freeze,
they petrify me. They may talk of a comet, or a burning   105
mountain, or some such bagatelle. But to me, a modest
woman, dressed out in all her finery, is the most tremendous object of the whole creation.

---

82 *The Englishman's malady* 'By Foreigners ... nervous *Distempers*, Spleen,
   Vapours, *and* Lowness of Spirits, *are in Derision, called the* ENGLISH
   MALADY' – George Cheyne, *The English Malady* (1733), p. i.

91 *of us* our sort

97 *rattle* chatter; see also III.i.322

105–6 *comet ... burning mountain* There was a brilliant comet in 1769 and a violent eruption of Vesuvius in 1767.

HASTINGS

Ha! ha! ha! At this rate, man, how can you ever expect to
marry?   110

MARLOW

Never, unless as among kings and princes, my bride were to
be courted by proxy. If, indeed, like an Eastern bridegroom,
one were to be introduced to a wife he never saw before, it
might be endured. But to go through all the terrors of a
formal courtship, together with the episode of aunts, grand-   115
mothers and cousins, and at last to blurt out the broad
staring question, of, 'Madam, will you marry me?' No, no,
that's a strain much above me I assure you.

HASTINGS

I pity you. But how do you intend behaving to the lady you
are come down to visit at the request of your father?   120

MARLOW

As I behave to all other ladies. Bow very low. Answer yes,
or no, to all her demands. – But for the rest, I don't think I
shall venture to look in her face, till I see my father's again.

HASTINGS

I'm surprised that one who is so warm a friend can be so
cool a lover.   125

MARLOW

To be explicit, my dear Hastings, my chief inducement
down was to be instrumental in forwarding your happiness,
not my own. Miss Neville loves you, the family don't know
you, as my friend you are sure of a reception, and let
honour do the rest.   130

HASTINGS

My dear Marlow! But I'll suppress the emotion. Were I a
wretch, meanly seeking to carry off a fortune, you should
be the last man in the world I would apply to for assistance.
But Miss Neville's person is all I ask, and that is mine, both
from her deceased father's consent, and her own incli-   135
nation.

MARLOW

Happy man! You have talents and art to captivate any
woman. I'm doomed to adore the sex, and yet to converse
with the only part of it I despise. This stammer in my

111–18 In Goldsmith's *Citizen of the World*, letter LXXII, the Chinese philosopher
    says if he were an Englishman he would probably be a bachelor. He could court
    a lady 'upon reasonable terms', but not her whole family, 'and then stand the
    butt of a whole country church'. *Works*, II 302.

114 *terrors* Q (terms L)

117 *staring* obvious

address, and this awkward prepossessing visage of mine,　140
can never permit me to soar above the reach of a milliner's
'prentice, or one of the duchesses of Drury Lane. Pshaw!
this fellow here to interrupt us.

Enter HARDCASTLE

HARDCASTLE
　Gentlemen, once more you are heartily welcome. Which is
　Mr Marlow? Sir, you're heartily welcome. It's not my way,　145
　you see, to receive my friends with my back to the fire. I like
　to give them a hearty reception in the old style at my gate.
　I like to see their horses and trunks taken care of.
MARLOW (*Aside*)
　He has got our names from the servants already. (*To him*)
　We approve your caution and hospitality, sir. (*To* HAST-　150
　INGS) I have been thinking, George, of changing our travel-
　ling dresses in the morning. I am grown confoundedly
　ashamed of mine.
HARDCASTLE
　I beg, Mr Marlow, you'll use no ceremony in this house.
HASTINGS
　I fancy, Charles, you're right: the first blow is half the　155
　battle. I intend opening the campaign with the white and
　gold.
HARDCASTLE
　Mr Marlow – Mr Hastings – gentlemen – pray be under no
　constraint in this house. This is Liberty Hall, gentlemen.
　You may do just as you please here.　160
MARLOW
　Yet, George, if we open the campaign too fiercely at first,

---

140 *prepossessing* Q (professing L): causing prejudice (*OED* 1)
141–2 *milliner's 'prentice* apprentice in the women's hats and fancy goods trade.
　　These girls had a dubious reputation; see Sheridan's *School for Scandal* (1777),
　　IV.iii.248–9.
142 *duchesses of Drury Lane* women of showy appearance connected with the
　　Theatre Royal, Drury Lane, as actresses or prostitutes
155 *Charles* L (George Q)
156–7 *campaign ... white and gold* advance on the ladies in white coat and gold
　　embroidered waistcoat; see ll. 163, 167 and notes below.
159 *Liberty Hall* Perhaps Goldsmith's own translation of *liberae sunt aedes*, words
　　with which old Periplectomenus welcomes young Pleusicles to his home (Plautus,
　　Miles Gloriosus, l. 678). In England the idea of liberty was associated with the
　　radical politician John Wilkes (1727–97).

we may want ammunition before it is over. I think to
reserve the embroidery to secure a retreat.

HARDCASTLE

Your talking of a retreat, Mr Marlow, puts me in mind of
the Duke of Marlborough, when he went to besiege   165
Denain. He first summoned the garrison –

MARLOW

Don't you think the *ventre d'or* waistcoat will do with the
plain brown?

HARDCASTLE

He first summoned the garrison, which might consist of
about five thousand men –   170

HASTINGS

I think not: brown and yellow mix but very poorly.

HARDCASTLE

I say, gentlemen, as I was telling you, he summoned the garrison, which might consist of about five thousand men –

MARLOW

The girls like finery.

HARDCASTLE

Which might consist of about five thousand men, well   175
appointed with stores, ammunition, and other implements
of war. Now, says the Duke of Marlborough, to George
Brooks, that stood next to him – you must have heard of
George Brooks – I'll pawn my Dukedom, says he, but I take
that garrison without spilling a drop of blood. So –   180

MARLOW

What, my good friend, if you gave us a glass of punch in the
meantime? It would help us to carry on the siege with
vigour.

HARDCASTLE

Punch, sir! (*Aside*) This is the most unaccountable kind of
modesty I ever met with.   185

---

163 *embroidery* embroidered clothes
     retreat. Q, Bell, Inchbald, Cooke (retreat. / Hast. And the Spring velvet brings up
     mine. L). This speech was evidently omitted in performance, so Hardcastle could
     pounce on 'retreat'.
165 *he* L, Bell, Inchbald, Cooke (we Q). Q was apparently corrected, as Hardcastle
     does not otherwise claim he was there. *Denain* was besieged in 1712 during the
     War of the Spanish Succession, but Marlborough did not take part; nor did
     Hardcastle, unless we are to suppose him aged about eighty.
166 *summoned* called to surrender (*OED* 5b)
167 *ventre d'or* gold-fronted
177–9 *George Brooks* Apparently not historical; certainly not famous.

MARLOW
Yes, sir, punch. A glass of warm punch, after our journey,
will be comfortable. This is Liberty Hall, you know.

HARDCASTLE
Here's cup, sir.

MARLOW (*Aside*)
So this fellow, in his Liberty Hall, will only let us have just
what he pleases.   190

HARDCASTLE (*Taking the cup*)
I hope you'll find it to your mind. I have prepared it with
my own hands, and I believe you'll own the ingredients are
tolerable. Will you be so good as to pledge me, sir? Here,
Mr Marlow, here is to our better acquaintance.   *Drinks*

MARLOW (*Aside*)
A very impudent fellow this! But he's a character, and I'll   195
humour him a little. Sir, my service to you.   *Drinks*

HASTINGS (*Aside*)
I see this fellow wants to give us his company, and forgets
that he's an innkeeper, before he has learned to be a gentleman.

MARLOW
From the excellence of your cup, my old friend, I suppose   200
you have a good deal of business in this part of the country.
Warm work, now and then, at elections, I suppose.

HARDCASTLE
No, sir, I have long given that work over. Since our betters
have hit upon the expedient of electing each other, there's
no business for us that sell ale.   205

HASTINGS
So, then you have no turn for politics I find.

HARDCASTLE
Not in the least. There was a time, indeed, I fretted myself
about the mistakes of government, like other people; but
finding myself every day growing more angry, and the gov-

---

188 *cup* wine and soda water mixed with such ingredients as sugar, spice and lemon,
     usually iced. Not as strong as punch; see note to I.ii.0 s.d.
202 *Warm work ... at elections* i.e. bribing voters with drinks paid for by the candi-
     dates
203–5 *Since ... ale*. Q (L brackets off and crosses out). Perhaps censored, as implying
     serious corruption. In some constituencies local landowners controlled
     elections.
205 *for us that sell ale* (Q italicises) i.e. for us who trade ale for votes; but the phrase
     confirms their idea that Hardcastle is an innkeeper
209 *growing* L (grow Q). Q spoils the antithesis ('growing more angry ... growing
     no better').

ernment growing no better, I left it to mend itself. Since 210
that, I no more trouble my head about Hyder Ali, or Ali
Cawn, than about Ally Croker. Sir, my service to you.

                                                    [*Drinks*]

HASTINGS
    So what with eating above stairs, and drinking below, with
    receiving your friends without, and amusing them within,
    you lead a good pleasant bustling life of it.   215

HARDCASTLE
    I do stir about a great deal, that's certain. Half the differ-
    ences of the parish are adjusted in this very parlour.

MARLOW (*After drinking*)
    And you have an argument in your cup, old gentleman,
    better than any in Westminster Hall.

HARDCASTLE
    Ay, young gentleman, that, and a little philosophy.   220

MARLOW (*Aside*)
    Well, this is the first time I ever heard of an innkeeper's
    philosophy.

HASTINGS
    So then, like an experienced general, you attack them on
    every quarter. If you find their reason manageable, you
    attack it with your philosophy; if you find they have no 225
    reason, you attack them with this. Here's your health, my
    philosopher.   *Drinks*

HARDCASTLE
    Good, very good, thank you; ha! ha! Your generalship puts
    me in mind of Prince Eugene, when he fought the Turks at
    the battle of Belgrade. You shall hear.   230

MARLOW
    Instead of the battle of Belgrade, I believe it's almost time

211–12 *Hyder Ali, or Ali Cawn* Q (Alli Bey, or Heider Ally; or Ally Cawn L). Hyder
    Ali and Mahomed Ali Khan were respectively rulers of Mysore and Bengal, when
    Clive and the historical Hastings were establishing British power in India.

212 *Ally Croker* character in a popular Irish song

213–14 *what ... without ... within* L (that ... within ... without Q). Hastings refers
    to their own reception, ll. 145–8 above.

219 *Westminster Hall* i.e. the London law courts

228 *ha! ha!* Q (ha! ha! ha! L). Perhaps Hardcastle is not amused.

231 *battle of Belgrade* Prince Eugene besieged Belgrade in 1717. Goldsmith had
    heard a description of the siege by General Oglethorpe (Boswell, 10 April 1772),
    so he – unlike Hardcastle – knew it was not strictly speaking a battle. See note
    to l. 165 above.

to talk about supper. What has your philosophy got in the house for supper?

HARDCASTLE

For supper, sir! (*Aside*) Was ever such a request to a man in his own house!   235

MARLOW

Yes, sir, supper sir; I begin to feel an appetite. I shall make devilish work tonight in the larder, I promise you.

HARDCASTLE (*Aside*)

Such a brazen dog sure never my eyes beheld. (*To him*) Why really, sir, as for supper I can't well tell. My Dorothy, and the cook maid, settle these things between them. I leave   240 these kind of things entirely to them.

MARLOW

You do, do you?

HARDCASTLE

Entirely. By the bye, I believe they are in actual consultation upon what's for supper this moment in the kitchen.

MARLOW

Then I beg they'll admit *me* as one of their privy council.   245 It's a way I have got. When I travel, I always choose to regulate my own supper. Let the cook be called. No offence I hope sir.

HARDCASTLE

Oh no, sir, none in the least; yet I don't know how: our Bridget, the cook maid, is not very communicative upon   250 these occasions. Should we send for her, she might scold us all out of the house.

HASTINGS

Let's see your list of the larder then. I ask it as a favour. I always match my appetite to my bill of fare.

MARLOW (*To* HARDCASTLE, *who looks at them with surprise*)

Sir, he's very right, and it's my way too.   255

HARDCASTLE

Sir, you have a right to command here. Here, Roger, bring us the bill of fare for tonight's supper. I believe it's drawn out. Your manner, Mr Hastings, puts me in mind of my uncle, Colonel Wallop. It was a saying of his, that no man was sure of his supper till he had eaten it.   260

---

232 *supper* a late evening meal

246 *way* Q (modest way L)

254 *bill of fare* list of available dishes. These prove too many and fancy for an inn, though not for a private house making a special effort.

256 *Here, Roger* Hardcastle calls to a servant offstage.

Enter ROGER, *who gives a bill of fare*

HASTINGS (*Aside*)
　All upon the high ropes! His uncle a colonel! We shall soon
　hear of his mother being a Justice of Peace. But let's hear
　the bill of fare.
MARLOW (*Perusing*)
　What's here? For the first course; for the second course; for
　the dessert. The devil, sir, do you think we have brought　265
　down the whole Joiners' Company, or the Corporation of
　Bedford, to eat up such a supper? Two or three little things,
　clean and comfortable, will do.
HASTINGS
　But, let's hear it.
MARLOW (*Reading*)
　For the first course at the top, a pig's face, and prune sauce.　270
HASTINGS
　Damn your pig's face, I say.
MARLOW
　And damn your prune sauce, say I.
HARDCASTLE
　And yet, gentlemen, to men that are hungry, a pig's face
　with prune sauce is very good eating.
MARLOW
　At the bottom, a calf's tongue and brains.　　　　　　　275
HASTINGS
　Let your brains be knocked out, my good sir; I don't like
　them.
MARLOW
　Or you may clap them on a plate by themselves. I do.
HARDCASTLE (*Aside*)
　Their impudence confounds me. (*To them*) Gentlemen, you
　are my guests, make what alterations you please. Is there　280
　anything else you wish to retrench or alter, gentlemen?

260　s.d. L (Q omits)
261　*All ... ropes*! Putting on airs!
266–7 *Joiners' Company ... Bedford* Trade guilds and town councils were famous for
　　banquets.
268　*clean* pure, simple
270, 275　*at the top, at the bottom* i.e. the positions of the dishes on the table
270, 271, 273　*pig's face, pig's face, a pig's face* L (pig, pig, pig Q): a country dish
　　made from a pig's head

MARLOW

Item. A pork pie, a boiled rabbit and sausages, a florentine,
a shaking pudding, and a dish of tiff-tuff-taffeta cream!

HASTINGS

Confound your made dishes, I shall be as much at a loss in
this house as at a green and yellow dinner at the French   285
ambassador's table. I'm for plain eating.

HARDCASTLE

I'm sorry, gentlemen, that I have nothing you like, but if
there be anything you have a particular fancy to –

MARLOW

Why, really, sir, your bill of fare is so exquisite, that any
one part of it is full as good as another. Send us what you   290
please. So much for supper. And now to see that our beds
are aired, and properly taken care of.

HARDCASTLE

I entreat that you'll leave all that to me. You shall not stir
a step.

MARLOW

Leave that to you! I protest, sir, you must excuse me, I   295
always look to these things myself.

HARDCASTLE

I must insist, sir, you'll make yourself easy on that head.

MARLOW

You see I'm resolved on it. (*Aside*) A very troublesome
fellow this, as ever I met with.

HARDCASTLE

Well, sir, I'm resolved at least to attend you. (*Aside*) This   300
may be modern modesty, but I never saw anything look so
like old-fashioned impudence.

282 *florentine* (probably) cheesecake. Name for various sweets and savouries; see
     Matthew Hamlyn, ed., *The Recipes of Hannah Woolley* (1988) pp. 122–3.

283 *shaking pudding* jelly, blancmange
     tuff L (taff Q). Presumably Marlow stutters; see l. 139 above.
     taffeta cream cream like taffeta, silky

284 *made dishes* dishes mixing several ingredients. Davis quotes Charlotte
     Cartwright, *The Lady's Best Companion* [1789]: 'made dishes are esteemed by
     the politest companies' (p. 26).

285 *green and yellow* Peter Dixon, in *Notes & Queries*, vol. 42 (1995) pp. 70–1,
     quotes *The Citizen of the World*, letter 78: 'I fancy the French would make the
     best cooks in the world, if they had but meat; as it is they can dress you out five
     different dishes from a nettle top, seven from a dock-leaf and twice as many from
     a frog's haunches'. Hence Dixon suggests Hastings thinks of green salads and
     yellow frogs' legs.

Exeunt MARLOW *and* HARDCASTLE

HASTINGS
So, I find this fellow's civilities begin to grow troublesome.
But who can be angry at those assiduities which are meant
to please him?   305

Enter MISS NEVILLE

Ha! what do I see? Miss Neville, by all that's happy!
MISS NEVILLE
My dear Hastings! To what unexpected good fortune, to
what accident am I to ascribe this happy meeting?
HASTINGS
Rather let me ask the same question, as I could never have
hoped to meet my dearest Constance at an inn.   310
MISS NEVILLE
An inn! Sure you mistake! My aunt, my guardian, lives
here. What could induce you to think this house an inn?
HASTINGS
My friend Mr Marlow, with whom I came down, and I,
have been sent here as to an inn, I assure you. A young
fellow whom we accidentally met at a house hard by   315
directed us hither.
MISS NEVILLE
Certainly it must be one of my hopeful cousin's tricks, of
whom you have heard me talk so often, ha! ha! ha! ha!
HASTINGS
He whom your aunt intends for you? He of whom I have
such just apprehensions?   320
MISS NEVILLE
You have nothing to fear from him, I assure you. You'd
adore him if you knew how heartily he despises me. My
aunt knows it too, and has undertaken to court me for him,
and actually begins to think she has made a conquest.
HASTINGS
Thou dear dissembler! You must know, my Constance, I   325
have just seized this happy opportunity of my friend's visit
here to get admittance into the family. The horses that
carried us down are now fatigued with their journey, but
they'll soon be refreshed; and then if my dearest girl will
trust in her faithful Hastings, we shall soon be landed in   330
France, where even among slaves the laws of marriage are
respected.

---

331 *slaves* Before the Revolution, the French were often called slaves; see *Works*, vol.
    II, pp. 28 and 464.

MISS NEVILLE

I have often told you, that though ready to obey you, I yet
should leave my little fortune behind with reluctance. The
greatest part of it was left me by my uncle, the India   335
Director, and chiefly consists in jewels. I have been for some
time persuading my aunt to let me wear them. I fancy I'm
very near succeeding. The instant they are put into my possession you shall find me ready to make them and myself
yours.   340

HASTINGS

Perish the baubles! Your person is all I desire. In the meantime, my friend Marlow must not be let into his mistake. I
know the strange reserve of his temper is such, that if
abruptly informed of it, he would instantly quit the house
before our plan was ripe for execution.   345

MISS NEVILLE

But how shall we keep him in the deception? Miss
Hardcastle is just returned from walking; what if we still
continue to deceive him? – This, this way –

They confer

Enter MARLOW

MARLOW

The assiduities of these good people tease me beyond bearing. My host seems to think it ill manners to leave me alone, 350
and so he claps not only himself but his old-fashioned wife
on my back. They talk of coming to sup with us too; and
then, I suppose, we are to run the gauntlet through all the
rest of the family. – What have we got here! –

HASTINGS

My dear Charles! Let me congratulate you! – The most for-   355
tunate accident! – Who do you think is just alighted?

MARLOW

Cannot guess.

HASTINGS

Our mistresses, boy, Miss Hardcastle and Miss Neville.
Give me leave to introduce Miss Constance Neville to your
acquaintance. Happening to dine in the neighbourhood,   360
they called on their return to take fresh horses here. Miss
Hardcastle has just stepped into the next room, and will be
back in an instant. Wasn't it lucky? eh?

335–6 *India Director* a Director of the East India Company
347–8 *we ... him?* Q (L omits)
358 *boy,* Q, Bell, Inchbald, Cooke (my boy. L)

MARLOW (*Aside*)
I have just been mortified enough of all conscience, and
here comes something to complete my embarrassment.   365
HASTINGS
Well! but wasn't it the most fortunate thing in the world?
MARLOW
Oh! yes. Very fortunate – a most joyful encounter. – But
our dresses, George, you know, are in disorder. – What if
we should postpone the happiness till tomorrow?
Tomorrow at her own house. – It will be every bit as   370
convenient – and rather more respectful. – Tomorrow let it
be.

Offering to go

MISS NEVILLE
By no means, sir. Your ceremony will displease her. The
disorder of your dress will show the ardour of your impatience. Besides, she knows you are in the house, and will   375
permit you to see her.
MARLOW
Oh! the devil! how shall I support it? Hem! hem! Hastings,
you must not go. You are to assist me, you know. I shall be
confoundedly ridiculous.
HASTINGS
Pshaw man! it's but the first plunge, and all's over. She's   380
but a woman, you know.
MARLOW
And of all women, she that I dread most to encounter! Yet,
hang it! I'll take courage. Hem!

Enter MISS HARDCASTLE *as returned from walking,
with a bonnet on, &c.*

HASTINGS (*Introducing them*)
Miss Hardcastle, Mr Marlow. I'm proud of bringing two
persons of such merit together, that only want to know, to   385
esteem each other.
MISS HARDCASTLE (*Aside*)
Now for meeting my modest gentleman with a demure face,
and quite in his own manner. (*After a pause, in which he
appears very uneasy and disconcerted*) I'm glad of your safe
arrival, sir. – I'm told you had some accidents on the way.   390

382–3 *Yet ... Hem!* ed. (L omits, Q adds to Marlow's previous speech). This emen-
    dation improves the logic of the dialogue.
383 s.d. *with a bonnet on* L (a Bonnet Q)
390 *on* L (by Q). L is unambiguous.

MARLOW
  Only a few madam. Yet we had some. Yes, madam, a good
  many accidents, but should be sorry – madam – or rather
  glad of any accidents – that are so agreeably concluded.
  Hem!

HASTINGS (*To him*)
  You never spoke better in your whole life. Keep it up, and   395
  I'll insure you the victory.

MISS HARDCASTLE
  I'm afraid you flatter, sir. You that have seen so much of
  the finest company can find little entertainment in an
  obscure corner of the country.

MARLOW (*Gathering courage*)
  I have lived, indeed, in the world, madam; but I have kept   400
  very little company. I have been but an observer upon life,
  madam, while others were enjoying it.

MISS NEVILLE
  But that, I am told, is the way to enjoy it at last.

HASTINGS (*To him*)
  Cicero never spoke better. Once more, and you are confirmed in assurance for ever.   405

MARLOW (*To him*)
  Hem! Stand by me then, and when I'm down, throw in a
  word or two to set me up again.

MISS HARDCASTLE
  An observer, like you, upon life, were, I fear, disagreeably
  employed, since you must have had much more to censure
  than to approve.   410

MARLOW
  Pardon me, madam. I was always willing to be amused. The
  folly of most people is rather an object of mirth than
  uneasiness.

HASTINGS (*To him*)
  Bravo, bravo. Never spoke so well in your whole life. (*To
  them*) Well! Miss Hardcastle, I see that you and Mr   415
  Marlow are going to be very good company. I believe our
  being here will but embarrass the interview.

MARLOW
  Not in the least, Mr Hastings. We like your company of all
  things. (*To him*) Zounds! George, sure you won't go? How
  can you leave us?   420

391 *Yet* L (Yes, Q). Marlow has said 'only a few' but wants to say 'a good many'.
396 *insure* guarantee (*OED* 5)
414–15 s.d. (*To them*) L (Q omits)

HASTINGS
Our presence will but spoil conversation, so we'll retire to
the next room. (*To him*) You don't consider, man, that we
are to manage a little tête-à-tête of our own.

Exeunt [HASTINGS *and* MISS NEVILLE]

MISS HARDCASTLE (*After a pause*)
But you have not been wholly an observer, I presume, sir:
the ladies, I should hope, have employed some part of your   425
addresses.

MARLOW (*Relapsing into timidity*)
Pardon me, madam, I – I – I – as yet have studied – only –
to – deserve them.

MISS HARDCASTLE
And that some say is the very worst way to obtain them.

MARLOW
Perhaps so, madam. But I love to converse only with the   430
more grave and sensible part of the sex. – But I'm afraid I
grow tiresome.

MISS HARDCASTLE
Not at all, sir; there is nothing I like so much as grave conversation myself; I could hear it for ever. Indeed I have
often been surprised how a man of *sentiment* could ever   435
admire those light airy pleasures, where nothing reaches the
heart.

MARLOW
It's – a disease – of the mind, madam. In the variety of
tastes there must be some who wanting a relish – for – um-
a-um.   440

MISS HARDCASTLE
I understand you, sir. There must be some, who wanting a
relish for refined pleasures, pretend to despise what they are
incapable of tasting.

MARLOW
My meaning, madam, but infinitely better expressed. And I
can't help observing – a –   445

---

427 *I – as yet* Q, Bell, Inchbald, Cooke (I – / Miss H. Then why take such pains to
  study and observe them? / Marlow. As yet I L). Marlow has not said he takes
  pains to study and observe the ladies; Miss Hardcastle's question seems
  shrewish, and was almost certainly cut in performance.

431 *sensible* having sensibility (*OED* 9a), appreciating sentiment; see ll. 435 and 481
  below, and notes

435 *sentiment* (italicised) Q (speculation L), thought prompted by feeling

MISS HARDCASTLE (*Aside*)
  Who could ever suppose this fellow impudent upon some
  occasions? (*To him*) You were going to observe, sir –
MARLOW
  I was observing, madam – I protest, madam, I forget what
  I was going to observe.
MISS HARDCASTLE (*Aside*)
  I vow and so do I. (*To him*) You were observing, sir, that   450
  in this age of hypocrisy – something about hypocrisy, sir.
MARLOW
  Yes, madam. In this age of hypocrisy, there are few who
  upon strict enquiry do not – a – a – a –
MISS HARDCASTLE
  I understand you perfectly, sir.
MARLOW (*Aside*)
  Egad! and that's more than I do myself.   455
MISS HARDCASTLE
  You mean that in this hypocritical age there are few that do
  not condemn in public what they practise in private, and
  think they pay every debt to virtue when they praise it.
MARLOW
  True, madam; those who have most virtue in their mouths,
  have least of it in their bosoms. But I'm sure I tire you,   460
  madam.
MISS HARDCASTLE
  Not in the least, sir; there's something so agreeable and
  spirited in your manner, such life and force. – Pray, sir, go
  on.
MARLOW
  Yes, madam. I was saying – that there are some occasions   465
  – when a total want of courage, madam, destroys all the –
  and puts us – upon a – a – a –
MISS HARDCASTLE
  I agree with you entirely, a want of courage upon some
  occasions assumes the appearance of ignorance, and
  betrays us when we most want to excel. I beg you'll pro-   470
  ceed.
MARLOW
  Yes, madam. Morally speaking, madam – But I see Miss
  Neville expecting us in the next room. I would not intrude
  for the world.
MISS HARDCASTLE
  I protest, sir, I never was more agreeably entertained in all   475
  my life. Pray go on.

MARLOW
Yes, madam. I was – But she beckons us to join her. Madam, shall I do myself the honour to attend you?

MISS HARDCASTLE
Well then, I'll follow.

MARLOW (*Aside*)
This pretty smooth dialogue has done for me.   *Exit*   480

MISS HARDCASTLE
Ha! ha! ha! Was there ever such a sober, sentimental interview? I'm certain he scarce looked in my face the whole time. Yet the fellow, but for his unaccountable bashfulness, is pretty well too. He has good sense, but then so buried in his fears, that it fatigues one more than ignorance. If I could   485 teach him a little confidence, it would be doing somebody that I know of a piece of service. But who is that somebody? – That, faith, is a question I can scarce answer.
                                                            Exit

Enter TONY *and* MISS NEVILLE, *followed by* MRS HARDCASTLE *and* HASTINGS

TONY
What do you follow me for, cousin Con? I wonder you're not ashamed to be so very engaging.   490

MISS NEVILLE
I hope, cousin, one may speak to one's own relations, and not be to blame.

TONY
Ay, but I know what sort of a relation you want to make me though; but it won't do. I tell you, cousin Con, it won't do, so I beg you'll keep your distance, I want no nearer   495 relationship.

She follows coquetting him to the back scene

MRS HARDCASTLE
Well! I vow, Mr Hastings, you are very entertaining. There's nothing in the world I love to talk of so much as London, and the fashions, though I was never there myself.

HASTINGS
Never there! You amaze me! From your air and manner, I   500

---

478 *attend* wait upon (his meaning?), wait for (her understanding)
481 *sentimental* full of sentiments, or sententious remarks
490 *engaging* inviting
496 s.d. *back scene* i.e. upstage

concluded you had been bred all your life either at
Ranelagh, St James's, or Tower Wharf.

MRS HARDCASTLE
Oh! Sir, you're only pleased to say so. We country persons
can have no manner at all. I'm in love with the town, and
that serves to raise me above some of our neighbouring rus-   505
tics; but who can have a manner, that has never seen the
Pantheon, the Grotto Gardens, the Borough, and such
places where the nobility chiefly resort? All I can do, is to
enjoy London at second-hand. I take care to know every
tête-à-tête from the *Scandalous Magazine*, and have all the   510
fashions, as they come out, in a letter from the two Miss
Rickets of Crooked Lane. Pray how do you like this head,
Mr Hastings?

HASTINGS
Extremely elegant and *dégagée*, upon my word, madam.
Your *friseur* is a Frenchman, I suppose?   515

MRS HARDCASTLE
I protest I dressed it myself from a print in the *Ladies'
Memorandum Book* for the last year.

HASTINGS
Indeed. Such a head in a side-box, at the playhouse, would
draw as many gazers as my Lady Mayoress at a City ball.

MRS HARDCASTLE
I vow, since inoculation began, there is no such thing to be   520

502 *Ranelagh ... Tower Wharf* Ranelagh (an entertainment centre) and St James's
    were fashionable places, but not Tower Wharf; Hastings mocks Mrs Hardcastle.
507–8 *Pantheon ... resort?* Only the recently opened Pantheon in Oxford Street was
    a place where the nobility resorted. The Grotto Gardens were less expensive than
    Ranelagh, and the Borough of Southwark had been taken over by rich trades-
    men.
510 *tête-à-tête ... Magazine* Each issue of the *Town and Country Magazine* carried
    an engraved portrait of a well known man and his mistress, captioned *tête-à-tête*,
    with a scandalous commentary.
512 *Crooked Lane* In *The Citizen of the World*, letter 71, Goldsmith implies that
    nobody 'above the degree of a cheesemonger' lived in this street.
    head elaborate hairdo
514 *dégagée* informal
515 *friseur* hairdresser
516–17 *Ladies' Memorandum Book* 'Twelve of the genteelest Head-dresses' were
    shown in the 1773 issue (Friedman).
518 *side-box* box at the side of the stage, where fashionable people were on show
520 *inoculation* i.e. against smallpox, a standard procedure for some fifty years

seen as a plain woman; so one must dress a little particular
or one may escape in the crowd.

HASTINGS

But that can never be your case, madam, in any dress.

Bowing

MRS HARDCASTLE

Yet, what signifies *my* dressing when I have such a piece of
antiquity by my side as Mr Hardcastle: all I can say will　525
never argue down a single button from his clothes. I have
often wanted him to throw off his great flaxen wig, and
where he was bald, to plaster it over like my Lord Pately,
with powder.

HASTINGS

You are right, madam; for, as among the ladies, there are　530
none ugly, so among the men there are none old.

MRS HARDCASTLE

But what do you think his answer was? Why, with his usual
gothic vivacity, he said I only wanted him to throw off his
wig to convert it into a *tête* for my own wearing.

HASTINGS

Intolerable! At your age you may wear what you please,　535
and it must become you.

MRS HARDCASTLE

Pray, Mr Hastings, what do you take to be the most fashionable age about town?

HASTINGS

Some time ago, forty was all the mode; but I'm told the
ladies intend to bring up fifty for the ensuing winter.　　540

MRS HARDCASTLE

Seriously? Then I shall be too young for the fashion.

HASTINGS

No lady begins now to put on jewels till she's past forty.
For instance, Miss there, in a polite circle, would be considered as a child, as a mere maker of samplers.

522　*escape* escape notice
526　*argue ... clothes* persuade him to dress fashionably. Hardcastle wears old-fash-
　　　ioned long coats and waistcoats.
526–9　Wearing wigs was going out of fashion, and powdering hair coming in.
528　*to plaster ... Pately,* Q (like my Lord Pately, to plaster it over L)
533　*gothic* medieval, barbaric, unfashionable; but a new fashion for things gothic
　　　had already started
534　*tête* head of hair
544　*samplers* beginners' exercises in embroidery

MRS HARDCASTLE
    And yet Mrs Niece thinks herself as much a woman, and is   545
    as fond of jewels, as the oldest of us all.
HASTINGS
    Your niece, is she? And that young gentleman, a brother of
    yours, I should presume?
MRS HARDCASTLE
    My son, sir. They are contracted to each other. Observe
    their little sports. They fall in and out ten times a day, as if   550
    they were man and wife already. (To them) Well Tony,
    child, what soft things are you saying to your cousin
    Constance this evening?
TONY
    I have been saying no soft things; but that it's very hard to
    be followed about so. Ecod! I've not a place in the house   555
    now that's left to myself but the stable.
MRS HARDCASTLE
    Never mind him, Con my dear. He's in another story
    behind your back.
MISS NEVILLE
    There's something generous in my cousin's manner. He
    falls out before faces to be forgiven in private.   560
TONY
    That's a damned confounded – crack.
MRS HARDCASTLE
    Ah! he's a sly one. Don't you think they're like each other
    about the mouth, Mr Hastings? The Blenkinsop mouth to
    a T. They're of a size too. Back to back, my pretties, that
    Mr Hastings may see you. Come Tony.   565
TONY
    You had as good not make me, I tell you.

                                                    Measuring

545 *Mrs* Q, Bell, Cooke (my L, Inchbald): pronounced 'Mistress', as applied to a
    young unmarried woman disapprovingly, and preferred to 'my' in the theatre.
550 *fall in and out* agree and disagree
557 *in another story* telling a different tale
561 *crack* lie (colloquial and euphemistic)
563 *Blenkinsop* Presumably Mrs Hardcastle's maiden name. In *The Vicar of
    Wakefield*, ch. xvii, 'the family of the Blenkinsops could never look strait before
    them'.
564–5 In *The Vicar of Wakefield*, ch. xvi, the vicar's wife, foolishly making a match
    between her daughter and Squire Thornhill, 'would sometimes tell the Squire
    that she thought him and Olivia extremely of a size, and would bid both stand
    up to see which was tallest'.

MISS NEVILLE
Oh lud! he has almost cracked my head.

MRS HARDCASTLE
Oh the monster! For shame, Tony. You a man, and behave so!

TONY
If I'm a man, let me have my fortin. Ecod! I'll not be made 570
a fool of no longer.

MRS HARDCASTLE
Is this, ungrateful boy, all I'm to get for the pains I have taken in your education? I that have rocked you in your cradle, and fed that pretty mouth with a spoon! Did not I work that waistcoat to make you genteel? Did not I pre- 575
scribe for you every day, and weep while the receipt was operating?

TONY
Ecod! you had reason to weep, for you have been dosing me ever since I was born. I have gone through every receipt in the *Complete Huswife* ten times over; and you have 580
thoughts of coursing me through *Quincy* next spring. But, Ecod! I tell you, I'll not be made a fool of no longer.

MRS HARDCASTLE
Wasn't it all for your good, viper? Wasn't it all for your good?

TONY
I wish you'd let me and my good alone then. Snubbing this 585
way when I'm in spirits. If I'm to have any good, let it come of itself; not to keep dinging it, dinging it into one so.

MRS HARDCASTLE
That's false; I never see you when you're in spirits. No, Tony, you then go to the alehouse or the kennel. I'm never

---

570 *fortin* fortune
572 *all I'm* L (all that I'm Q). L is more forceful.
574–81 *Did not I ... next spring.* Q (L omits)
575 *work* embroider; John Quick as Lumpkin wore a ridiculously elaborate waist-coat in the first production
576 *receipt* prescribed remedy
580–1 *The Complete Housewife* and John Quincy's *Complete English Dispensatory* were popular books on home management and medicine; 'huswife' was pro-nounced 'huziff'.
583 *viper* alluding to the proverbial warning against nourishing a viper in your bosom
585 *I* Q (Ecod, I L)
589 *the kennel* L (kennel Q) i.e. he goes to be with his dogs

to be delighted with your agreeable, wild notes, unfeeling 590
monster!

TONY

Ecod! Mamma, your own notes are the wildest of the two.

MRS HARDCASTLE

Was ever the like? But I see he wants to break my heart, I
see he does.

HASTINGS

Dear madam, permit me to lecture the young gentleman a 595
little. I'm certain I can persuade him to his duty.

MRS HARDCASTLE

Well! I must retire. Come, Constance, my love. You see Mr
Hastings, the wretchedness of my situation: was ever poor
woman so plagued with a dear, sweet, pretty, provoking,
undutiful boy.   600

Exeunt MRS HARDCASTLE *and* MISS NEVILLE

TONY (*Singing*)

'There was a young man riding by, and fain would have his
will. Rang do didlo dee'. Don't mind her. Let her cry. It's
the comfort of her heart. I have seen her and sister cry over
a book for an hour together, and they said, they liked the
book the better the more it made them cry.   605

HASTINGS

Then you're no friend to the ladies, I find, my pretty young
gentleman?

TONY

That's as I find 'em.

HASTINGS

Not to her of your mother's choosing, I dare answer? And
yet she appears to me a pretty well-tempered girl.   610

TONY

That's because you don't know her as well as I. Ecod! I
know every inch about her; and there's not a more bitter
cantankerous toad in all Christendom.

HASTINGS (*Aside*)

Pretty encouragement, this, for a lover!

TONY

I have seen her since the height of that. She has as many   615
tricks as a hare in a thicket, or a colt the first day's breaking.

---

590 *wild notes* Recalls Milton's idea of Shakespeare warbling 'his native wood-notes
      wild' (*L'Allegro*, 133–4).
601–2 *(Singing)* 'There ... dee'. Q (L omits). The source, if any, of these 'wild notes'
      has not been found.
610 *pretty* fairly

HASTINGS
    To me she appears sensible and silent!
TONY
    Ay, before company. But when she's with her play-mates
    she's as loud as a hog in a gate.   620
HASTINGS
    But there is a meek modesty about her that charms me.
TONY
    Yes, but curb her never so little, she kicks up, and you're
    flung in a ditch.
HASTINGS
    Well, but you must allow her a little beauty. – Yes, you
    must allow her some beauty.   625
TONY
    Bandbox! She's all a made up thing, mun. Ah! could you
    but see Bet Bouncer of these parts, you might then talk of
    beauty. Ecod, she has two eyes as black as sloes, and cheeks
    as broad and red as a pulpit cushion. She'd make two of
    she.   630
HASTINGS
    Well, what say you to a friend that would take this bitter
    bargain off your hands?
TONY
    Anon?
HASTINGS
    Would you thank him that would take Miss Neville and
    leave you to happiness and your dear Betsy?   635
TONY
    Ay; but where is there such a friend, for who would take
    her?
HASTINGS
    I am he. If you but assist me, I'll engage to whip her off to
    France, and you shall never hear more of her.
TONY
    Assist you! Ecod I will, to the last drop of my blood. I'll   640
    clap a pair of horses to your chaise that shall trundle you
    off in a twinkling. And maybe get you a part of her fortin
    besides, in jewels, that you little dream of.
HASTINGS
    My dear Squire, this looks like a lad of spirit.

620 *in a gate* stuck in a gate
626 *Bandbox* artificial; prettified with millinery from her bandbox
633 *Anon?* Come again?
643 *besides* L (beside Q)

TONY

Come along then, and you shall see more of my spirit 645
before you have done with me. (*Singing*) 'We are the boys,
that fears no noise, where the thundering cannons roar'.

Exeunt

Act III

Enter HARDCASTLE

HARDCASTLE

What could my old friend Sir Charles mean by recom-
mending his son as the modestest young man in town? To
me he appears the most impudent piece of brass that ever
spoke with a tongue. He has taken possession of the easy
chair by the fireside already. He took off his boots in the   5
parlour, and desired me to see them taken care of. I'm
desirous to know how his impudence affects my daughter.
– She will certainly be shocked at it.

Enter MISS HARDCASTLE, *plainly dressed*

Well, my Kate, I see you have changed your dress as I bid
you; and yet, I believe, there was no great occasion.   10

MISS HARDCASTLE

I find such a pleasure, sir, in obeying your commands, that
I take care to observe them without ever debating their pro-
priety.

HARDCASTLE

And yet, Kate, I sometimes give you some cause, particularly when I recommended my *modest* gentleman to you as   15
a lover today.

MISS HARDCASTLE

You taught me to expect something extraordinary, and I
find the original exceeds the description.

HARDCASTLE

I was never so surprised in my life! He has quite confounded all my faculties!   20

MISS HARDCASTLE

I never saw anything like it: and a man of the world too!

HARDCASTLE

Ay, he learned it all abroad. – What a fool was I, to think

646–7 'We ... roar' Q, L (substantially). As at 601–2 the source has not been found.
  3 *brass* shameless effrontery; see also ll. 35 and 78 below

a young man could learn modesty by travelling. He might
as soon learn wit at a masquerade.

MISS HARDCASTLE

It seems all natural to him.   25

HARDCASTLE

A good deal assisted by bad company and a French dancing-master.

MISS HARDCASTLE

Sure you mistake, papa! A French dancing-master could
never have taught him that timid look, – that awkward
address, – that bashful manner –   30

HARDCASTLE

Whose look? whose manner? child!

MISS HARDCASTLE

Mr Marlow's: his *mauvaise honte*, his timidity struck me at
the first sight.

HARDCASTLE

Then your first sight deceived you; for I think him one of
the most brazen first sights that ever astonished my senses. 35

MISS HARDCASTLE

Sure, sir, you rally! I never saw anyone so modest.

HARDCASTLE

And can you be serious? I never saw such a bouncing swaggering puppy since I was born. Bully Dawson was but a
fool to him.

MISS HARDCASTLE

Surprising! He met me with a respectful bow, a stammering 40
voice, and a look fixed on the ground.

HARDCASTLE

He met me with a loud voice, a lordly air, and a familiarity
that froze me to death.

MISS HARDCASTLE

He treated me with diffidence and respect; censured the
manners of the age; admired the prudence of girls that   45
never laughed; tired me with apologies for being tiresome;
then left the room with a bow, and, 'Madam, I would not
for the world detain you'.

---

32 *mauvaise honte* bashfulness

36 *rally* joke

38 *Bully Dawson* Theophilus Lucas, in *Memoirs of the Most Famous Gamesters*
(1714), says 'This Fellow was a noted Bully about *London* for many Years, and
was also as noted a Coward' (p. 40).

43 *froze me to death* L, Bell, Inchbald (made my blood freeze again Q, Cooke). He
echoes his daughter's words at I.i.129.

HARDCASTLE
He spoke to me as if he knew me all his life before. Asked
twenty questions, and never waited for an answer.   50
Interrupted my best remarks with some silly pun, and when
I was in my best story of the Duke of Marlborough and
Prince Eugene, he asked if I had not a good hand at making
punch. Yes, Kate, he asked your father if he was a maker of
punch!   55

MISS HARDCASTLE
One of us must certainly be mistaken.

HARDCASTLE
If he be what he has shown himself, I'm determined he shall
never have my consent.

MISS HARDCASTLE
And if he be the sullen thing I take him, he shall never have
mine.   60

HARDCASTLE
In one thing then we are agreed – to reject him.

MISS HARDCASTLE
Yes. But upon conditions. For if you should find him less
impudent, and I more presuming; if you find him more
respectful, and I more importunate – I don't know – the
fellow is well enough for a man. – Certainly we don't meet   65
many such at a horse race in the country.

HARDCASTLE
If we should find him so. – But that's impossible. The first
appearance has done my business. I'm seldom deceived in
that.

MISS HARDCASTLE
And yet there may be many good qualities under that first   70
appearance.

HARDCASTLE
Ay, when a girl finds a fellow's outside to her taste, she then
sets about guessing the rest of his furniture. With her, a
smooth face stands for good sense, and a genteel figure for
every virtue.   75

52–3 *in my … he asked* Q (talking of my Friend Bruce, ask'd me L). An audience
    would remember Brooks (II.i.177–9) no better than Goldsmith himself appar-
    ently did.
65–6 *we … country* Q, Bell, Cooke (he has a very passable complexion L,
    Inchbald). It seems Q was generally preferred in the theatre.
73 *furniture* Q (qualifications L) i.e. what he has inside. At l. 370 below Hardcastle
    queries Marlow's 'qualifications', but here 'outside' suggests 'furniture', as if a
    house were being discussed.

MISS HARDCASTLE

I hope, sir, a conversation begun with a compliment to my good sense won't end with a sneer at my understanding?

HARDCASTLE

Pardon me, Kate. But if young Mr Brazen can find the art of reconciling contradictions, he may please us both, perhaps.　　　　　　80

MISS HARDCASTLE

And as one of us must be mistaken, what if we go to make further discoveries?

HARDCASTLE

Agreed. But depend on't I'm in the right.

MISS HARDCASTLE

And depend on't I'm not much in the wrong.

Exeunt

Enter TONY *running in with a casket*

TONY

Ecod! I have got them. Here they are. My cousin Con's 85 necklaces, bobs and all. My mother shan't cheat the poor souls out of their fortune neither. Oh! my genus, is that you?

Enter HASTINGS

HASTINGS

My dear friend, how have you managed with your mother? I hope you have amused her with pretending love for your 90 cousin, and that you are willing to be reconciled at last? Our horses will be refreshed in a short time, and we shall soon be ready to set off.

TONY

And here's something to bear your charges by the way (*giving the casket*). Your sweetheart's jewels. Keep them, 95 and hang those, I say, that would rob you of one of them.

HASTINGS

But how have you procured them from your mother?

TONY

Ask me no questions, and I'll tell you no fibs. I procured them by the rule of thumb. If I had not a key to every drawer in my mother's bureau, how could I go to the ale- 100 house so often as I do? An honest man may rob himself of his own at any time.

---

86 *bobs* pendants
90 *amused* bemused, deceived
99 *rule of thumb* rough and ready method

HASTINGS

Thousands do it every day. But to be plain with you, Miss
Neville is endeavouring to procure them from her aunt this
very instant. If she succeeds, it will be the most delicate way   105
at least of obtaining them.

TONY

Well, keep them, till you know how it will be. But I know
how it will be well enough, she'd as soon part with the only
sound tooth in her head.

HASTINGS

But I dread the effects of her resentment, when she finds she   110
has lost them.

TONY

Never you mind her resentment, leave *me* to manage that.
I don't value her resentment the bounce of a cracker.
Zounds! here they are. Morris! Prance!

Exit HASTINGS

Enter MRS HARDCASTLE, MISS NEVILLE

MRS HARDCASTLE

Indeed, Constance, you amaze me. Such a girl as you want   115
jewels? It will be time enough for jewels, my dear, twenty
years hence, when your beauty begins to want repairs.

MISS NEVILLE

But what will repair beauty at forty, will certainly improve
it at twenty, madam.

MRS HARDCASTLE

Yours, my dear, can admit of none. That natural blush is   120
beyond a thousand ornaments. Besides, child, jewels are
quite out at present. Don't you see half the ladies of our
acquaintance, my Lady Killdaylight, and Mrs Crump, and
the rest of them, carry their jewels to town, and bring
nothing but paste and marcasites back.   125

MISS NEVILLE

But who knows, madam, that somebody that shall be
nameless would like me best with all my little finery about
me?

---

113 *bounce of a cracker* sound of a backside (Partridge)
114 *Morris! Prance!* Get a move on! Gee up!
114 s.d. *Enter* MRS L (TONY, Mrs. Q)
123 *Killdaylight* suggests sleeping by day and sparkling by night; *Crump* suggests
    crooked, hunched up
124–5 *bring … back* bring back only imitation jewels; having perhaps pawned their
    real ones, unsuspected of Mrs Hardcastle

MRS HARDCASTLE
Consult your glass, my dear, and then see, if with such a
pair of eyes, you want any better sparklers. What do you   130
think, Tony, my dear, does your cousin Con want any
jewels, in your eyes, to set off her beauty?

TONY
That's as thereafter may be.

MISS NEVILLE
My dear aunt, if you knew how it would oblige me.

MRS HARDCASTLE
A parcel of old-fashioned rose and table-cut things. They   135
would make you look like the court of King Solomon at a
puppet-show. Besides, I believe I can't readily come at
them. They may be missing for aught I know to the contrary.

TONY (*Apart to* MRS HARDCASTLE)
Then why don't you tell her so at once, as she's so longing   140
for them. Tell her they're lost. It's the only way to quiet her.
Say they're lost, and call me to bear witness.

MRS HARDCASTLE (*Apart to* TONY)
You know, my dear, I'm only keeping them for you. So if I
say they're gone, you'll bear me witness, will you? He! he!
he!   145

TONY
Never fear me! Ecod! I'll say I saw them taken out with my
own eyes.

MISS NEVILLE
I desire them but for a day, madam. Just to be permitted to
show them as relics, and then they may be locked up again.

MRS HARDCASTLE
To be plain with you, my dear Constance, if I could find   150
them, you should have them. They're missing, I assure you.
Lost, for aught I know; but we must have patience
wherever they are.

MISS NEVILLE
I'll not believe it; this is but a shallow pretence to deny me.
I know they're too valuable to be so slightly kept, and as   155
you are to answer for the loss.

MRS HARDCASTLE
Don't be alarmed, Constance. If they be lost, I must restore
an equivalent. But my son knows they are missing, and not
to be found.

---

135 *parcel* collection; disparaging, as at I.ii.14 and l. 275 below
    rose and table-cut rather crudely cut
149 *relics* mementoes

TONY

    That I can bear witness to. They are missing, and not to be   160
found, I'll take my oath on't.

MRS HARDCASTLE

    You must learn resignation, my dear; for though we lose
our fortune, yet we should not lose our patience. See me,
how calm I am.

MISS NEVILLE

    Ay, people are generally calm at the misfortunes of others.   165

MRS HARDCASTLE

    Now, I wonder a girl of your good sense should waste a
thought upon such trumpery. We shall soon find them; and,
in the meantime, you shall make use of my garnets till your
jewels be found.

MISS NEVILLE

    I detest garnets.   170

MRS HARDCASTLE

    The most becoming things in the world to set off a clear
complexion. You have often seen how well they look upon
me. You *shall* have them.

MISS NEVILLE

    I dislike them of all things. You shan't stir –

                           Exit MRS HARDCASTLE

    Was ever anything so provoking, to mislay my own jewels,   175
and force me to wear her trumpery.

TONY

    Don't be a fool. If she gives you the garnets, take what you
can get. The jewels are your own already. I have stolen
them out of her bureau, and she does not know it. Fly to
your spark, he'll tell you more of the matter. Leave me to   180
manage *her*.

MISS NEVILLE

    My dear cousin!

TONY

    Vanish! She's here, and has missed them already.

                          [*Exit* MISS NEVILLE]

---

167 *trumpery* see note to I.i.19
168 *garnets* comparatively cheap jewels
174 s.d. ed. (Q has it after Mrs Hardcastle's speech). Miss Neville tries to stop her
      exit.
180 *spark* lover
183 s.d. ed. (Q omits). Tony hastens Miss Neville's exit, perhaps hearing his mother
      crying 'Thieves! Robbers!' offstage.

Zounds! how she fidgets and spits about like a Catharine
wheel.   185

Enter MRS HARDCASTLE

MRS HARDCASTLE

Confusion! thieves! robbers! We are cheated, plundered,
broke open, undone.

TONY

What's the matter, what's the matter, mamma? I hope
nothing has happened to any of the good family!

MRS HARDCASTLE

We are robbed. My bureau has been broke open, the jewels   190
taken out, and I'm undone.

TONY

Oh! is that all? Ha! ha! ha! By the laws, I never saw it better
acted in my life. Ecod, I thought you was ruined in earnest,
ha! ha! ha!

MRS HARDCASTLE

Why boy, I *am* ruined in earnest. My bureau has been   195
broke open, and all taken away.

TONY

Stick to that; ha! ha! ha! stick to that, I'll bear witness, you
know, call me to bear witness.

MRS HARDCASTLE

I tell you, Tony, by all that's precious, the jewels are gone,
and I shall be ruined for ever.   200

TONY

Sure I know they're gone, and I am to say so.

MRS HARDCASTLE

My dearest Tony, but hear me. They're gone, I say.

TONY

By the laws, mamma, you make me for to laugh, ha! ha! I
know who took them well enough, ha! ha! ha!

MRS HARDCASTLE

Was there ever such a blockhead, that can't tell the differ-   205
ence between jest and earnest. I tell you I'm not in jest,
booby.

TONY

That's right, that's right: you must be in a bitter passion,
and then nobody will suspect either of us. I'll bear witness
that they are gone.   210

MRS HARDCASTLE

Was there ever such a cross-grained brute, that won't hear

184–5 *Catharine wheel* rotating firework
211 *cross-grained* see note to I.ii.102–3

me! Can you bear witness that you're no better than a fool?
Was ever poor woman so beset with fools on one hand, and
thieves on the other!

TONY

I can bear witness to that.   215

MRS HARDCASTLE

Bear witness again, you blockhead you, and I'll turn you
out of the room directly. My poor niece, what will become
of *her*! Do you laugh, you unfeeling brute, as if you enjoyed
my distress.

TONY

I can bear witness to that.   220

MRS HARDCASTLE

Do you insult me, monster? I'll teach you to vex your
mother, I will.

TONY

I can bear witness to that.

> *He runs off, she follows him*

> *Enter* MISS HARDCASTLE *and* MAID

MISS HARDCASTLE

What an unaccountable creature is that brother of mine, to
send them to the house as an inn, ha! ha! I don't wonder at   225
his impudence.

MAID

But what is more, madam, the young gentleman as you
passed by in your present dress, asked me if you were the
barmaid? He mistook you for the barmaid, madam.

MISS HARDCASTLE

Did he? Then as I live I'm resolved to keep up the delusion. 230
Tell me, Pimple, how do you like my present dress? Don't
you think I look something like Cherry in *The Beaux'
Stratagem*?

MAID

It's the dress, madam, that every lady wears in the country,
but when she visits or receives company.   235

MISS HARDCASTLE

And are you sure he does not remember my face or person?

MAID

Certain of it.

---

223 s.d. Q (*Exit. Mrs H. follows, pushing him* L)

226 *his* i.e. Marlow's

232–3 *Cherry . . . Stratagem* The Landlord's daughter in Farquhar's well-known play,
   a witty girl who aims at marrying a gentleman, without success.

MISS HARDCASTLE

I vow I thought so; for though we spoke for some time together, yet his fears were such, that he never once looked up during the interview. Indeed, if he had, my bonnet 240 would have kept him from seeing me.

MAID

But what do you hope from keeping him in his mistake?

MISS HARDCASTLE

In the first place, I shall be *seen*, and that is no small advantage to a girl who brings her face to market. Then I shall perhaps make an acquaintance, and that's no small victory 245 gained over one who never addresses any but the wildest of her sex. But my chief aim is to take my gentleman off his guard, and like an invisible champion of romance examine the giant's force before I offer to combat.

MAID

But are you sure you can act your part, and disguise your 250 voice, so that he may mistake that, as he has already mistaken your person?

MISS HARDCASTLE

Never fear me. I think I have got the true bar cant. – Did your honour call? – Attend the Lion there. – Pipes and tobacco for the Angel. – The Lamb has been outrageous 255 this half hour.

MAID

It will do, madam. But he's here.   *Exit*

Enter MARLOW

MARLOW

What a bawling in every part of the house; I have scarce a moment's repose. If I go to the best room, there I find my host and his story. If I fly to the gallery, there we have my 260 hostess with her curtsy down to the ground. I have at last got a moment to myself, and now for recollection.

                                        Walks and muses

MISS HARDCASTLE

Did you call, sir? Did your honour call?

MARLOW (*Musing*)

As for Miss Hardcastle, she's too grave and sentimental for me.   265

254–5 *Lion ... Angel ... Lamb* Rooms at inns were given such names.
255 *outrageous* clamorous

MISS HARDCASTLE
Did your honour call?

She still places herself before him, he turning away

MARLOW
No, child. (*Musing*) Besides from the glimpse I had of her, I think she squints.

MISS HARDCASTLE
I'm sure, sir, I heard the bell ring.

MARLOW
No, no. (*Musing*) I have pleased my father, however, by   270
coming down, and I'll tomorrow please myself by return-
ing.

Taking out his tablets, and perusing

MISS HARDCASTLE
Perhaps the other gentleman called, sir.

MARLOW
I tell you, no.

MISS HARDCASTLE
I should be glad to know, sir. We have such a parcel of ser-   275
vants.

MARLOW
No, no, I tell you. (*Looks full in her face*) Yes, child, I think
I did call. I wanted – I wanted – I vow, child, you are vastly
handsome.

MISS HARDCASTLE
Oh la, sir, you'll make one ashamed.   280

MARLOW
Never saw a more sprightly malicious eye. Yes, yes, my
dear, I did call. Have you got any of your – a – what-d'ye-
call-it in the house?

MISS HARDCASTLE
No, sir, we have been out of that these ten days.

MARLOW
One may call in this house, I find, to very little purpose.   285
Suppose I should call for a taste, just by way of trial, of the
nectar of your lips; perhaps I might be disappointed of that
too.

MISS HARDCASTLE
Nectar! nectar! That's a liquor there's no call for in these
parts. French, I suppose. We keep no French wines here, sir.   290

---

266 s.d. *still* continually
272 s.d. *tablets* notebook
275 *parcel* see note to l. 135 above
281 *malicious* mischievous
287 *of* L (in Q). Marlow fears he won't get a kiss, not that he won't like one.

MARLOW
Of true English growth, I assure you.

MISS HARDCASTLE
Then it's odd I should not know it. We brew all sorts of wines in this house, and I have lived here these eighteen years.

MARLOW
Eighteen years! Why one would think, child, you kept the   295
bar before you were born. How old are you?

MISS HARDCASTLE
Oh! sir, I must not tell my age. They say women and music should never be dated.

MARLOW
To guess at this distance, you can't be much above forty (*approaching*). Yet nearer I don't think so much (*approach-*   300
ing). By coming close to some women they look younger still; but when we come very close indeed (*attempting to kiss her*) –

MISS HARDCASTLE
Pray, sir, keep your distance. One would think you wanted to know one's age as they do horses, by mark of mouth.

MARLOW
I protest, child, you use me extremely ill. If you keep me at   305
this distance, how is it possible you and I can be ever acquainted?

MISS HARDCASTLE
And who wants to be acquainted with you? I want no such acquaintance, not I. I'm sure you did not treat Miss Hardcastle that was here awhile ago in this obstropalous   310
manner. I'll warrant me, before her you looked dashed, and kept bowing to the ground, and talked, for all the world, as if you was before a Justice of Peace.

MARLOW (*Aside*)
Egad! she has hit it, sure enough. (*To her*) In awe of her, child? Ha! ha! ha! A mere, awkward, squinting thing, no,   315
no. I find you don't know me. I laughed, and rallied her a little; but I was unwilling to be too severe. No, I could not be too severe, *curse me*!

MISS HARDCASTLE
Oh! then, sir, you are a favourite, I find, among the ladies?

---

304 *mark of mouth* mark on the incisor teeth, showing a horse's age
310 *obstropalous* obstreperous (colloquial)
318 *curse me!* Q (curse me. L): perhaps in italics to emphasise its affectation. Marlow is now so anxious to avoid talking as if before a Justice of Peace, that he rattles away as if at the Ladies' Club (see ll. 321–2 below, and notes).

MARLOW

    Yes, my dear, a great favourite. And yet, hang me, I don't   320
see what they find in me to follow. At the Ladies' Club in
town, I'm called their agreeable Rattle. Rattle, child, is not
my real name, but one I'm known by. My name is
Solomons. Mr Solomons, my dear, at your service (*offering
to salute her*).

MISS HARDCASTLE

    Hold, sir; you were introducing me to your club, not to   325
yourself. And you're so great a favourite there, you say?

MARLOW

    Yes, my dear. There's Mrs Mantrap, Lady Betty Blackleg,
the Countess of Sligo, Mrs Longhorns, old Miss Biddy
Buckskin, and your humble servant, keep up the spirit of
the place.   330

MISS HARDCASTLE

    Then it's a very merry place, I suppose.

MARLOW

    Yes, as merry as cards, suppers, wine, and old women can
make us.

MISS HARDCASTLE

    And their agreeable Rattle, ha! ha! ha!

MARLOW (*Aside*)

    Egad! I don't quite like this chit. She looks knowing,   335
methinks. [*To her*] You laugh, child!

MISS HARDCASTLE

    I can't but laugh to think what time they all have for mind-
ing their work or their family.

MARLOW (*Aside*)

    All's well, she don't laugh at me. (*To her*) Do *you* ever
work, child?   340

321 *Ladies' Club* a fashionable London club, with both men and women members
322 *Rattle* i.e. conversationalist, chatterer. At the Turk's Head Club on 7 May 1773
    Goldsmith himself 'rattled away as usual' (Boswell).
323–4 *name ... dear*, Q (own name is L)
324 s.d. *salute* kiss
327–8 *Mrs Mantrap ... Sligo* Mantrap suggests an amorous widow; a blackleg was
    a cardsharper or betting swindler; the Countess of Sligo (an Irish county) is an
    invented title.
328 *Longhorns* L, Bell, Inchbald, Cooke (Langhorns Q)
328–9 *Biddy Buckskin* Q (Rachael Buck-skin L) refers to Rachael Lloyd, a leading
    member of the club
335 *chit* young or small girl (colloquial and pejorative); see note to I.ii.107
338 *work* needlework
    family Q (families L)

MISS HARDCASTLE
Ay, sure. There's not a screen or a quilt in the whole house
but what can bear witness to that.

MARLOW
Odso! Then you must show me your embroidery. I embroider and draw patterns myself a little. If you want a judge of
your work you must apply to me.   345

Seizing her hand

MISS HARDCASTLE
Ay, but the colours don't look well by candlelight. You
shall see all in the morning.

Struggling

MARLOW
And why not now, my angel? Such beauty fires beyond the
power of resistance.

Enter HARDCASTLE, *who stands in surprise*

Pshaw! the father here! My old luck: I never nicked seven   350
that I did not throw ames ace three times following.   *Exit*

HARDCASTLE
So, madam! So I find *this* is your *modest* lover. This is your
humble admirer that kept his eyes fixed on the ground, and
only adored at humble distance. Kate, Kate, art thou not
ashamed to deceive thy father so?   355

MISS HARDCASTLE
Never trust me, dear papa, but he's still the modest man I
first took him for, you'll be convinced of it as well as I.

HARDCASTLE
By the hand of my body I believe his impudence is infec-
tious! Didn't I see him seize your hand? Didn't I see him
haul you about like a milkmaid? And now you talk of his   360
respect and his modesty, forsooth!

MISS HARDCASTLE
But if I shortly convince you of his modesty, that he has
only the faults that will pass off with time, and the virtues
that will improve with age, I hope you'll forgive him.

HARDCASTLE
The girl would actually make one run mad! I tell you I'll   365
not be convinced. I am convinced. He has scarcely been
three hours in the house, and he has already encroached on

---

343 *Odso!* mild expression of surprise
349 s.d. ed. (Q has it after Marlow's speech)
350–1 *nicked seven … following* threw a winner without throwing three losers after-
       wards; *ames ace* both aces (ones), the lowest possible score
355 *thy* L (your Q)

all my prerogatives. You may like his impudence, and call
it modesty. But my son-in-law, madam, must have very different qualifications.   370

MISS HARDCASTLE
Sir, I ask but this night to convince you.

HARDCASTLE
You shall not have half the time, for I have thoughts of
turning him out this very hour.

MISS HARDCASTLE
Give me that hour then, and I hope to satisfy you.

HARDCASTLE
Well, an hour let it be then. But I'll have no trifling with 375
your father. All fair and open do you mind me.

MISS HARDCASTLE
I hope, sir, you have ever found that I considered your commands as my pride; for your kindness is such, that my duty
as yet has been inclination.

Exeunt

Act IV

Enter HASTINGS *and* MISS NEVILLE

HASTINGS
You surprise me! Sir Charles Marlow expected here this
night? Where have you had your information?

MISS NEVILLE
You may depend upon it. I just saw his letter to Mr
Hardcastle, in which he tells him he intends setting out a
few hours after his son.   5

HASTINGS
Then, my Constance, all must be completed before he
arrives. He knows me; and should he find me here, would
discover my name, and perhaps my designs, to the rest of
the family.

MISS NEVILLE
The jewels, I hope, are safe.   10

HASTINGS
Yes, yes. I have sent them to Marlow, who keeps the keys
of our baggage. In the meantime, I'll go to prepare matters
for our elopement. I have had the Squire's promise of a

8 *discover* disclose. Hastings forgets Hardcastle knows his name (II.i.158).

fresh pair of horses; and, if I should not see him again, will
write him further directions.   *Exit*   15

MISS NEVILLE

Well! success attend you. In the meantime, I'll go amuse my
aunt with the old pretence of a violent passion for my
cousin.   *Exit*

Enter MARLOW, *followed by a* SERVANT

MARLOW

I wonder what Hastings could mean by sending me so valuable a thing as a casket to keep for him, when he knows the   20
only place I have is the seat of a post-coach at an inn door.
Have you deposited the casket with the landlady, as I
ordered you? Have you put it into her own hands?

SERVANT

Yes, your honour.

MARLOW

She said she'd keep it safe, did she?   25

SERVANT

Yes, she said she'd keep it safe enough; she asked me how
I came by it, and she said she had a great mind to make me
give an account of myself.   *Exit*

MARLOW

Ha! ha! ha! They're safe however. What an unaccountable
set of beings have we got amongst! This little barmaid   30
though runs in my head most strangely, and drives out the
absurdities of all the rest of the family. She's mine, she must
be mine, or I'm greatly mistaken.

Enter HASTINGS

HASTINGS

Bless me! I quite forgot to tell her that I intended to prepare
at the bottom of the garden. Marlow here, and in spirits   35
too!

MARLOW

Give me joy, George! Crown me, shadow me with laurels!
Well, George, after all, we modest fellows don't want for
success among the women.

HASTINGS

Some women you mean. But what success has your   40
honour's modesty been crowned with now, that it grows so
insolent upon us?

MARLOW
  Didn't you see the tempting, brisk, lovely, little thing that
  runs about the house with a bunch of keys to its girdle?
HASTINGS
  Well! and what then?   45
MARLOW
  She's mine, you rogue you. Such fire, such motion, such
  eyes, such lips – but, egad! she would not let me kiss them
  though.
HASTINGS
  But are you so sure, so very sure of her?
MARLOW
  Why man, she talked of showing me her work above-stairs,   50
  and I am to improve the pattern.
HASTINGS
  But how can *you*, Charles, go about to rob a woman of her
  honour?
MARLOW
  Pshaw! pshaw! we all know the honour of the barmaid of
  an inn. I don't intend to *rob* her, take my word for it,   55
  there's nothing in this house I shan't honestly *pay* for.
HASTINGS
  I believe the girl has virtue.
MARLOW
  And if she has, I should be the last man in the world that
  would attempt to corrupt it.
HASTINGS
  You have taken care, I hope, of the casket I sent you to lock 60
  up? It's in safety?
MARLOW
  Yes, yes. It's safe enough. I have taken care of it. But how
  could you think the seat of a post-coach, at an inn door, a
  place of safety? Ah! numbskull! I have taken better precau-
  tions for you than you did for yourself. – I have –   65
HASTINGS
  What?
MARLOW
  I have sent it to the landlady to keep for you.
HASTINGS
  To the landlady?
MARLOW
  The landlady.

---

  43 *brisk* lively, perhaps wanton
  50 *above-stairs* upstairs, in her bedroom

HASTINGS
  You did!   70
MARLOW
  I did. She's to be answerable for its forthcoming, you know.
HASTINGS
  Yes, she'll bring it forth, with a witness.
MARLOW
  Wasn't I right? I believe you'll allow that I acted prudently
  upon this occasion?
HASTINGS (*Aside*)
  He must not see my uneasiness.   75
MARLOW
  You seem a little disconcerted though, methinks. Sure,
  nothing has happened?
HASTINGS
  No, nothing. Never was in better spirits in all my life. And
  so you left it with the landlady, who, no doubt, very read-
  ily undertook the charge?   80
MARLOW
  Rather too readily. For she not only kept the casket, but,
  through her great precaution, was going to keep the mes-
  senger too. Ha! ha! ha!
HASTINGS
  He! he! he! They're safe however.
MARLOW
  As a guinea in a miser's purse.   85
HASTINGS (*Aside*)
  So now all hopes of fortune are at an end, and we must set
  off without it. (*To him*) Well, Charles, I'll leave you to your
  meditations on the pretty barmaid, and, he! he! he! may
  you be as successful for yourself as you have been for me.

Exit

MARLOW
  Thank ye, George! I ask no more. Ha! ha! ha!   90

Enter HARDCASTLE

HARDCASTLE
  I no longer known my own house. It's turned all topsy-
  turvy. His servants have got drunk already. I'll bear it no
  longer, and yet, from my respect for his father, I'll be calm.
  (*To him*) Mr Marlow, your servant. I'm your very humble
  servant.   95

72 *with a witness* with a vengeance
76 *Sure* Surely

Bowing low

MARLOW

 Sir, your humble servant. (*Aside*) What's to be the wonder
 now?

HARDCASTLE

 I believe, sir, you must be sensible, sir, that no man alive
 ought to be more welcome than your father's son, sir. I
 hope you think so.   100

MARLOW

 I do from my soul, sir. I don't want much entreaty. I generally make my father's son welcome wherever he goes.

HARDCASTLE

 I believe you do, from my soul, sir. But though I say
 nothing to your own conduct, that of your servants is insuf-
 ferable. Their manner of drinking is setting a very bad 105
 example in this house, I assure you.

MARLOW

 I protest, my very good sir, that's no fault of mine. If they
 don't drink as they ought *they* are to blame. I ordered them
 not to spare the cellar. I did, I assure you. (*To the side
 scene*) Here, let one of my servants come up. (*To him*) My 110
 positive directions were, that as I did not drink myself, they
 should make up for my deficiencies below.

HARDCASTLE

 Then they had your orders for what they do! I'm satisfied!

MARLOW

 They had, I assure you. You shall hear from one of themselves.   115

Enter SERVANT [JEREMY] *drunk*

MARLOW

 You, Jeremy! Come forward, sirrah! What were my orders?
 Were you not told to drink freely, and call for what you
 thought fit, for the good of the house?

HARDCASTLE (*Aside*)

 I begin to lose my patience.

JEREMY

 Please your honour, liberty and Fleet Street for ever! 120
 Though I'm but a servant, I'm as good as another man. I'll

---

114 *assure you* L (assure Q)

120 *liberty ... ever* A slogan, or drunken version of one, associated with Wilkes; see
  also II.i.159. Fleet Street was not at this time synonymous with journalism, but
  a bookseller living there had been pilloried for selling Wilkes's paper *The North
  Briton*, No. 45, which had been banned.

drink for no man before supper, sir, damn me! Good liquor
will sit upon a good supper, but a good supper will not sit
upon – hiccup – upon my conscience, sir.   [*Exit*]

MARLOW

You see, my old friend, the fellow is as drunk as he can   125
possibly be. I don't know what you'd have more, unless
you'd have the poor devil soused in a beer barrel.

HARDCASTLE

Zounds! he'll drive me distracted if I contain myself any
longer. Mr Marlow, sir; I have submitted to your insolence
for more than four hours, and I see no likelihood of its   130
coming to an end. I'm now resolved to be master here, sir,
and I desire that you and your drunken pack may leave my
house directly.

MARLOW

Leave your house! – Sure you jest, my good friend? What,
when I'm doing what I can to please you?   135

HARDCASTLE

I tell you, sir, you don't please me; so I desire you'll leave
my house.

MARLOW

Sure you cannot be serious? At this time o' night, and such
a night. You only mean to banter me?

HARDCASTLE

I tell you, sir, I'm serious; and, now that my passions are   140
roused, I say this house is mine, sir; this house is mine, and
I command you to leave it directly.

MARLOW

Ha! ha! ha! A puddle in a storm. I shan't stir a step, I assure
you. (*In a serious tone*) This, your house, fellow! It's my
house. This is my house. Mine, while I choose to stay. What   145
right have you to bid me leave this house, sir? I never met
with such impudence, curse me, never in my whole life
before.

HARDCASTLE

Nor I, confound me if ever I did. To come to my house, to
call for what he likes, to turn me out of my own chair, to   150
insult the family, to order his servants to get drunk, and
then to tell me 'This house is mine, sir'. By all that's impudent it makes me laugh. Ha! ha! ha! Pray sir, (*bantering*) as
you take the house, what think you of taking the rest of the
furniture? There's a pair of silver candlesticks, and there's 155

---

122 *damn me* ed. (dammy Q, damme L)
143 *A puddle in a storm* i.e. fancy an innkeeper getting so angry

a firescreen, and here's a pair of brazen-nosed bellows, perhaps you may take a fancy to them?

MARLOW

Bring me your bill, sir, bring me your bill, and let's make
no more words about it.

HARDCASTLE

There are a set of prints too. What think you of *The Rake's*   160
Progress for your own apartment?

MARLOW

Bring me your bill, I say; and I'll leave you and your infer-
nal house directly.

HARDCASTLE

Then there's a mahogany table, that you may see your own
face in.   165

MARLOW

My bill, I say.

HARDCASTLE

I had forgot the great chair, for your own particular slum-
bers, after a hearty meal.

MARLOW

Zounds! bring me my bill, I say, and let's hear no more
on't.   170

HARDCASTLE

Young man, young man, from your father's letter to me, I
was taught to expect a well-bred modest man, as a visitor
here, but now I find him no better than a coxcomb and a
bully; but he will be down here presently, and shall hear
more of it.   *Exit*   175

MARLOW

How's this? Sure I have not mistaken the house? Everything
looks like an inn. The servants cry, 'Coming'. The atten-
dance is awkward. The barmaid, too, to attend us.

Enter MISS HARDCASTLE

But she's here, and will further inform me. Whither so fast,
child? A word with you.   180

MISS HARDCASTLE

Let it be short then. I'm in a hurry. (*Aside*) I believe he
begins to find out his mistake, but it's too soon quite to
undeceive him.

MARLOW

Pray, child, answer me one question. What are you, and
what may your business in this house be?   185

160–1 *The Rake's Progress* a famous series of pictures by Hogarth (1735)
175 s.d. ed. (Q has it after Marlow's speech)

MISS HARDCASTLE
A relation of the family, sir.

MARLOW
What, a poor relation?

MISS HARDCASTLE
Yes, sir. A poor relation. Appointed to keep the keys, and
to see that the guests want nothing in my power to give
them.   190

MARLOW
That is, you act as the barmaid of this inn.

MISS HARDCASTLE
Inn! – Oh law! – What brought that in your head? One of
the best families in the county, keep an inn? Ha! ha! ha! old
Mr Hardcastle's house an inn!

MARLOW
Mr Hardcastle's house! Is this house Mr Hardcastle's   195
house, child?

MISS HARDCASTLE
Ay, sure. Whose else should it be?

MARLOW
So then, all's out, and I have been damnably imposed on.
Oh, confound my stupid head, I shall be laughed at over the
whole town. I shall be stuck up in *caricatura* in all the print   200
shops. The *Dullissimo Macaroni*. To mistake this house of
all others for an inn, and my father's old friend for an
innkeeper. What a swaggering puppy must he take me for.
What a silly puppy do I find myself. There again, may I be
hanged, my dear, but I mistook you for the barmaid.   205

MISS HARDCASTLE
Dear me! dear me! I'm sure there's nothing in my *behavour*
to put me upon a level with one of that stamp.

MARLOW
Nothing, my dear, nothing. But I was in for a list of blun-
ders, and could not help making you a subscriber. My stupidity saw everything the wrong way. I mistook your   210
assiduity for assurance, and your simplicity for allurement.
But it's over – this house I no more show *my* face in.

---

192 *law!* Lord! (vulgar)

195 *this house* Q (this L)

199-200 *the whole town* London

200–1 *I shall ... Macaroni* Macaronis, young men who affected Italian taste, were
    often caricatured in prints; he fears being represented as the dullest of them all.

206 *behavour* Q (behaviour L). The Q spelling and italics may show she still speaks
    like an uneducated girl; see ll. 192 above, 218 below, and notes.

MISS HARDCASTLE
    I hope, sir, I have done nothing to disoblige you. I'm sure I
    should be sorry to affront any gentleman who has been so
    polite, and said so many civil things to me. I'm sure I should   215
    be sorry (*pretending to cry*) if he left the family upon my
    account. I'm sure I should be sorry people said anything
    amiss, since I have no fortin but my charackter.
MARLOW (*Aside*)
    By heaven, she weeps. This is the first mark of tenderness I
    ever had from a modest woman, and it touches me. (*To*   220
    her) Excuse me, my lovely girl, you are the only part of the
    family I leave with reluctance. But to be plain with you, the
    difference of our birth, fortune and education, make an
    honourable connexion impossible; and I can never harbour
    a thought of seducing simplicity that trusted in my honour,   225
    or bringing ruin upon one, whose only fault was being too
    lovely.
MISS HARDCASTLE (*Aside*)
    Generous man! I now begin to admire him. (*To him*) But
    I'm sure my family is as good as Miss Hardcastle's, and
    though I'm poor, that's no great misfortune to a contented   230
    mind, and, until this moment, I never thought that it was
    bad to want fortune.
MARLOW
    And why now, my pretty simplicity?
MISS HARDCASTLE
    Because it puts me at a distance from one, that if I had a
    thousand pound I would give it all to.   235
MARLOW (*Aside*)
    This simplicity bewitches me, so that if I stay I'm undone. I
    must make one bold effort, and leave her. (*To her*) Your
    partiality in my favour, my dear, touches me most sensibly,
    and were I to live for myself alone, I could easily fix my
    choice. But I owe too much to the opinion of the world, too   240
    much to the authority of a father, so that – I can scarcely
    speak it – it affects me. Farewell.   *Exit*

---

218 *fortin* L (fortune Q)
     charackter L (character Q)
220 *touches me* Q, Bell, Inchbald, Cooke (touches me. How natural it is for a Recluse
     to fall in love at first. L). Perhaps L should have read 'at first sight', but this self-
     justification seems to have been cut in the theatre.
230 *though* Q, Bell, Inchbald, Cooke (I'm not behind her in Plain-work and Pastry.
     What tho' L). Perhaps cut because the idea of Miss Hardcastle as pastrycook was
     too ridiculous.

MISS HARDCASTLE

I never knew half his merit till now. He shall not go, if I have power or art to detain him. I'll still preserve the character in which I stooped to conquer, but will undeceive my 245 papa, who, perhaps, may laugh him out of his resolution.

Exit

Enter TONY, MISS NEVILLE

TONY

Ay, you may steal for yourselves the next time, I have done my duty. She has got the jewels again, that's a sure thing; but she believes it was all a mistake of the servants.

MISS NEVILLE

But, my dear cousin, sure you won't forsake us in this distress? If she in the least suspects that I am going off, I shall certainly be locked up, or sent to my aunt Pedigree's, which is ten times worse. 250

TONY

To be sure, aunts of all kinds are damned bad things. But what can I do? I have got you a pair of horses that will fly 255 like Whistlejacket, and I'm sure you can't say but I have courted you nicely before her face. Here she comes, we must court a bit or two more, for fear she should suspect us.

They retire, and seem to fondle

Enter MRS HARDCASTLE

MRS HARDCASTLE

Well, I was greatly fluttered, to be sure. But my son tells me 260 it was all a mistake of the servants. I shan't be easy, however, till they are fairly married, and then let her keep her own fortune. But what do I see! Fondling together, as I'm alive. I never saw Tony so sprightly before. Ah! have I caught you, my pretty doves? What, billing, exchanging 265 stolen glances, and broken murmurs? Ah!

TONY

As for murmurs, mother, we grumble a little now and then, to be sure. But there's no love lost between us.

---

245 *stooped to conquer* Q (conquered L)

256 *Whistlejacket* a famous racehorse

258 *bit* Q (stroke L)

268 *no love lost* (to Tony and Miss Neville) no love wasted on each other; (to Mrs Hardcastle) no love lost by grumbling

MRS HARDCASTLE
A mere sprinkling, Tony, upon the flame, only to make it
burn brighter.   270
MISS NEVILLE
Cousin Tony promises to give us more of his company at
home. Indeed, he shan't leave us any more. It won't leave
us, cousin Tony, will it?
TONY
Oh! it's a pretty creature. No, I'd sooner leave my horse in
a pound, than leave you when you smile upon one so. Your   275
laugh makes you so becoming.
MISS NEVILLE
Agreeable cousin! Who can help admiring that natural
humour, that pleasant, broad, red, thoughtless – (*patting
his cheek*) Ah! it's a bold face.
MRS HARDCASTLE
Pretty innocence.   280
TONY
I'm sure I always loved cousin Con's hazel eyes, and her
pretty long fingers, that she twists this way and that, over
the haspicholls, like a parcel of bobbins.
MRS HARDCASTLE
Ah, he would charm the bird from the tree. I was never so
happy before. My boy takes after his father, poor Mr   285
Lumpkin, exactly. The jewels, my dear Con, shall be yours
incontinently. You shall have them. Isn't he a sweet boy,
my dear? You shall be married tomorrow, and we'll put off
the rest of his education, like Dr Drowsy's sermons, to a
fitter opportunity.   290

Enter DIGGORY

DIGGORY
Where's the Squire? I have got a letter for your worship.
TONY
Give it to my mamma. She reads all my letters first.
DIGGORY
I had orders to deliver it into your own hands.

---

274 *leave* Q, Bell, Inchbald, Cooke (leave a hare in her form, the dogs in full cry, or
L): L was used in the first performance, but a critic asked, 'Would not one of the
similes be quite sufficient?' so the hare simile was omitted; see *Letters*, p. xl.
275 *pound* enclosure for strays
283 *haspicholls* harpsichord (colloquial)
like ... bobbins (probably) like a lot of spools used in lace making; this flight of
fancy baffles Mrs Hardcastle
287 *incontinently* immediately

TONY
    Who does it come from?
DIGGORY
    Your worship mun ask that o' the letter itself.   [*Exit*]   295
TONY
    I could wish to know, though.

                            Turning the letter, and gazing on it

MISS NEVILLE (*Aside*)
    Undone, undone. A letter to him from Hastings. I know the
    hand. If my aunt sees it, we are ruined for ever. I'll keep her
    employed a little if I can. (*To* MRS HARDCASTLE) But I have
    not told you, madam, of my cousin's smart answer just now   300
    to Mr Marlow. We so laughed! You must know, madam –
    this way a little, for he must not hear us.

                                            They confer

TONY (*Still gazing*)
    A damned cramp piece of penmanship, as ever I saw in my
    life. I can read your print hand very well. But here there are
    such handles, and shanks, and dashes, that one can scarce   305
    tell the head from the tail. 'To Anthony Lumpkin, Esquire'.
    It's very odd, I can read the outside of my letters, where my
    own name is, well enough. But when I come to open it, it's
    all – buzz. That's hard, very hard; for the inside of the letter
    is always the cream of the correspondence.   310
MRS HARDCASTLE
    Ha! ha! ha! Very well, very well. And so my son was too
    hard for the philosopher.
MISS NEVILLE
    Yes, madam; but you must hear the rest, madam. A little
    more this way, or he may hear us. You'll hear how he puz-
    zled him again.   315
MRS HARDCASTLE
    He seems strangely puzzled now himself, methinks.
TONY (*Still gazing*)
    A damned up and down hand, as if it was disguised in
    liquor. (*Reading*) 'Dear Sir'. Ay, that's that. Then there's an
    M, and a T, and an S, but whether the next be an izzard or
    an R, confound me, I cannot tell.   320
MRS HARDCASTLE
    What's that, my dear? Can I give you any assistance?

304 *print hand* handwriting like print
305 *handles, and shanks* loops above and below the line
318 *Sir* Q (Squire L). Perhaps not a misprint; Tony can't read.
319 *izzard* letter z

MISS NEVILLE
Pray, aunt, let me read it. Nobody reads a cramp hand
better than I (*twitching the letter from her*). Do you know
who it is from?

TONY
Can't tell, except from Dick Ginger the feeder.   325

MISS NEVILLE
Ay, so it is. (*Pretending to read*) 'Dear Squire, Hoping that
you're in health, as I am at this present. The gentlemen of
the Shake-bag club has cut the gentlemen of Goose-green
quite out of feather. The odds – um – odd battle – um –
long fighting' – um here, here, it's all about cocks, and   330
fighting; it's of no consequence, here, put it up, put it up.
              Thrusting the crumpled letter upon him

TONY
But I tell you, miss, it's of all the consequence in the world.
I would not lose the rest of it for a guinea. Here, mother,
do you make it out. Of no consequence!

              Giving MRS HARDCASTLE *the letter*

MRS HARDCASTLE
How's this! (*Reads*) 'Dear Squire, I'm now waiting for Miss   335
Neville, with a post-chaise and pair, at the bottom of the
garden, but I find my horses yet unable to perform the journey. I expect you'll assist us with a pair of fresh horses, as
you promised. Dispatch is necessary, as the *hag*' – ay the
hag – 'your mother, will otherwise suspect us. Yours,   340
Hastings'! Grant me patience! I shall run distracted! My
rage chokes me!

MISS NEVILLE
I hope, madam, you'll suspend your resentment for a few
moments, and not impute to me any impertinence, or sinis-
ter design that belongs to another.   345

MRS HARDCASTLE (*Curtsying very low*)
Fine spoken, madam, you are most miraculously polite and
engaging, and quite the very pink of courtesy and circum-
spection, madam. (*Changing her tone*) And you, you great
ill-fashioned oaf, with scarce sense enough to keep your
mouth shut, were you too joined against me? But I'll defeat   350
all your plots in a moment. As for you, madam, since you

---

325 *feeder* trainer of fighting-cocks
328 *Shake-bag* large fighting-cock
    Goose-green goose-turd or yellowy green; presumably the cock's colour
328–9 *has cut . . . feather* have deplumed, deflated
331 *put it up* pocket it

have got a pair of fresh horses ready, it would be cruel to
disappoint them. So, if you please, instead of running away
with your spark, prepare this very moment, to run off with
me. Your old aunt Pedigree will keep you secure, I'll war- 355
rant me. You too, sir, may mount your horse, and guard us
upon the way. Here, Thomas, Roger, Diggory! I'll show
you, that I wish you better than you do yourselves. *Exit*

MISS NEVILLE
So now I'm completely ruined.

TONY
Ay, that's a sure thing. 360

MISS NEVILLE
What better could be expected from being connected with
such a stupid fool, and after all the nods and signs I made
him.

TONY
By the laws, miss, it was your own cleverness, and not my
stupidity, that did your business. You were so nice and so 365
busy with your Shake-bags and Goose-greens, that I
thought you could never be making believe.

Enter HASTINGS

HASTINGS
So, sir, I find by my servant, that you have shown my letter,
and betrayed us. Was this well done, young gentleman?

TONY
Here's another. Ask Miss there who betrayed you. Ecod, it 370
was her doing, not mine.

Enter MARLOW

MARLOW
So, I have been finely used here among you. Rendered contemptible, driven into ill manners, despised, insulted,
laughed at.

TONY
Here's another. We shall have old Bedlam broke loose pres- 375
ently.

MISS NEVILLE
And there, sir, is the gentleman to whom we all owe every
obligation.

---

365 *nice* 'superfluously exact' (Johnson)
375 *old Bedlam broke loose* a complete outbreak of madness; Bedlam or Bethlehem
   Hospital was the well known London asylum

MARLOW

What can I say to him, a mere boy, an idiot, whose ignorance and age are a protection?   380

HASTINGS

A poor contemptible booby, that would but disgrace correction.

MISS NEVILLE

Yet with cunning and malice enough to make himself merry with all our embarrassments.

HASTINGS

An insensible cub.   385

MARLOW

Replete with tricks and mischief.

TONY

Baw! damn me, but I'll fight you both one after the other – with baskets.

MARLOW

As for him, he's below resentment. But your conduct, Mr Hastings, requires an explanation. You knew of my mistakes, yet would not undeceive me.   390

HASTINGS

Tortured as I am with my own disappointments, is this a time for explanations? It is not friendly, Mr Marlow.

MARLOW

But, sir –

MISS NEVILLE

Mr Marlow, we never kept on your mistakes, till it was too   395
late to undeceive you. Be pacified.

Enter SERVANT

SERVANT

My mistress desires you'll get ready immediately, madam. The horses are putting to. Your hat and things are in the next room. We are to go thirty miles before morning.

MISS NEVILLE

Well, well; I'll come presently.   400

Exit SERVANT

380 *protection* i.e. against a challenge to a duel
381–2 *correction* i.e. by being killed or injured in a duel
388 *baskets* basket-hilted swords, used for exercise
395 *mistakes* L (mistake Q). Marlow says 'mistakes' at l. 390–1 above.
396 s.d. *Enter* Q (*Enter a* L)
398 *putting to* being attached to the coach
400 s.d. ed. (Q has it after the servant's speech)

MARLOW (*To* HASTINGS)
Was it well done, sir, to assist in rendering me ridiculous?
To hang me out for the scorn of all my acquaintance?
Depend upon it, sir, I shall expect an explanation.

HASTINGS
Was it well done, sir, if you're upon that subject, to deliver
what I entrusted to yourself, to the care of another, sir?   405

MISS NEVILLE
Mr Hastings! Mr Marlow! Why will you increase my distress by this groundless dispute? I implore, I entreat you –

Enter SERVANT

SERVANT
Your cloak, madam. My mistress is impatient.   [*Exit*]

MISS NEVILLE
I come. [*To* HASTINGS *and* MARLOW] Pray be pacified. If I
leave you thus, I shall die with apprehension.   410

Enter SERVANT

SERVANT
Your fan, muff, and gloves, madam. The horses are waiting.   [*Exit*]

MISS NEVILLE
Oh, Mr Marlow! If you knew what a scene of constraint
and ill-nature lies before me, I'm sure it would convert your
resentment into pity.   415

MARLOW
I'm so distracted with a variety of passions, that I don't
know what I do. Forgive me, madam. George, forgive me.
You know my hasty temper, and should not exasperate it.

HASTINGS
The torture of my situation is my only excuse.

MISS NEVILLE
Well, my dear Hastings, if you have that esteem for me that   420
I think – that I am sure you have, your constancy for three
years will but increase the happiness of our future connexion. If –

---

407 s.d. *Enter* Q (*Enter a* L). L may imply a different servant; see note to l. 396
above.

410 s.d. Q (L omits). Hence Q has three entries for a servant or servants, and L only
two. Both texts are unsatisfactory, as no exits are marked except after the first
entry. To create a sense of mad haste, three entries seem better than two, but perhaps all by the same servant.

421–2 *for three years* i.e. till she is twenty-one, and of an age to marry without Mrs
Hardcastle's consent

MRS HARDCASTLE (*Within*)
 Miss Neville! Constance, why Constance, I say!
MISS NEVILLE
 I'm coming. Well, constancy. Remember, constancy is the   425
 word.   *Exit*
HASTINGS
 My heart! How can I support this? To be so near happi-
 ness, and such happiness.
MARLOW (*To* TONY)
 You see now, young gentleman, the effects of your folly.
 What might be amusement to you, is here disappointment,   430
 and even distress.
TONY (*From a reverie*)
 Ecod, I have hit it. It's here. Your hands. Yours and yours,
 my poor sulky. My boots there, ho! Meet me two hours
 hence at the bottom of the garden; and if you don't find
 Tony Lumpkin a more good-natured fellow than you   435
 thought for, I'll give you leave to take my best horse, and
 Bet Bouncer into the bargain. Come along. My boots, ho!

                                                   Exeunt

Act V, [Scene i]

Enter HASTINGS *and* SERVANT

HASTINGS
 You saw the old lady and Miss Neville drive off, you say?
SERVANT
 Yes, your honour. They went off in a post-coach, and the
 young Squire went on horseback. They're thirty miles off
 by this time.
HASTINGS
 Then all my hopes are over.   5
SERVANT
 Yes, sir. Old Sir Charles is arrived. He and the old gentle-

---

432 *I have ... here* Recalls Iago hatching his plots: 'I ha't. It is engendered' (*Othello*,
     I.iii.385); ''Tis here, but yet confused' (II.i.292).
     here i.e. in his head
433 *sulky* i.e. the more aloof Marlow? But it is the unhappy Hastings who is to meet
     him in the garden.
436-7 *take ... bargain* Q, Bell, Inchbald, Cooke (run me through the guts with a
     shoulder of mutton L). L is consistent with Tony's thinking at V.ii.44-9, but
     may have been considered too 'low', and evidently Q was usually played.

man of the house have been laughing at Mr Marlow's mistake this half hour. They are coming this way.

HASTINGS
Then I must not be seen. So now to my fruitless appointment at the bottom of the garden. This is about the time.   10

Exeunt

Enter SIR CHARLES *and* HARDCASTLE

HARDCASTLE
Ha! ha! ha! The peremptory tone in which he sent forth his sublime commands!

SIR CHARLES
And the reserve with which I suppose he treated all your advances!

HARDCASTLE
And yet he might have seen something in me above a   15
common innkeeper, too.

SIR CHARLES
Yes, Dick, but his mistook you for an uncommon innkeeper, ha! ha! ha!

HARDCASTLE
Well, I'm in too good spirits to think of anything but joy. Yes, my dear friend, this union of our families will make   20
our personal friendships hereditary; and though my daughter's fortune is but small –

SIR CHARLES
Why, Dick, will you talk of fortune to *me*? My son is possessed of more than a competence already, and can want nothing but a good and virtuous girl to share his happiness   25
and increase it. If they like each other, as you say they do –

HARDCASTLE
If, man? I tell you they *do* like each other. My daughter as good as told me so.

SIR CHARLES
But girls are apt to flatter themselves, you know.

HARDCASTLE
I saw him grasp her hand in the warmest manner myself;   30
and here he comes to put you out of your *ifs*, I warrant him.

Enter MARLOW

MARLOW
I come, sir, once more, to ask pardon for my strange

conduct. I can scarce reflect on my insolence without confusion.

HARDCASTLE

Tut, boy, a trifle. You take it too gravely. An hour or two's   35
laughing with my daughter will set all to rights again. She'll
never like you the worse for it.

MARLOW

Sir, I shall be always proud of her approbation.

HARDCASTLE

Approbation is but a cold word, Mr Marlow; if I am not
deceived, you have something more than approbation   40
thereabouts. You take me?

MARLOW

Really, sir, I have not that happiness.

HARDCASTLE

Come, boy, I'm an old fellow, and know what's what, as
well as you that are younger. I know what has passed
between you; but mum!   45

MARLOW

Sure, sir, nothing has passed between us but the most pro-
found respect on my side, and the most distant reserve on
hers. You don't think, sir, that my impudence has been
passed upon all the rest of the family?

HARDCASTLE

Impudence! No, I don't say that – not quite impudence.   50
Though girls like to be played with, and rumpled a little too
sometimes. But she has told no tales, I assure you.

MARLOW

I never gave her the slightest cause.

HARDCASTLE

Well, well, I like modesty in its place well enough. But this
is over-acting, young gentleman. You *may* be open. Your   55
father and I will like you the better for it.

MARLOW

May I die, sir, if I ever –

HARDCASTLE

I tell you, she don't dislike you; and as I'm sure you like
her –

MARLOW

Dear sir – I protest, sir –   60

HARDCASTLE

I see no reason why you should not be joined as fast as the
parson can tie you.

41 *take* understand
50 s.p. HARDCASTLE L (*Miss* HARDCASTLE Q)

MARLOW
But hear me, sir –

HARDCASTLE
Your father approves the match, I admire it, every
moment's delay will be doing mischief, so –   65

MARLOW
But why won't you hear me? By all that's just and true, I
never gave Miss Hardcastle the slightest mark of my attachment, or even the most distant hint to suspect me of affection. We had but one interview, and that was formal,
modest and uninteresting.   70

HARDCASTLE (*Aside*)
This fellow's formal modest impudence is beyond bearing.

SIR CHARLES
And you never grasped her hand, or made any protesta-
tions?

MARLOW
As heaven is my witness, I came down in obedience to your
commands. I saw the lady without emotion, and parted   75
without reluctance. I hope you'll exact no further proofs of
my duty, nor prevent me from leaving a house in which I
suffer so many mortifications.   *Exit*

SIR CHARLES
I'm astonished at the air of sincerity with which he parted.

HARDCASTLE
And I'm astonished at the deliberate intrepidity of his assur-   80
ance.

SIR CHARLES
I dare pledge my life and honour upon his truth.

HARDCASTLE
Here comes my daughter, and I would stake my happiness
upon her veracity.

Enter MISS HARDCASTLE

Kate, come hither, child. Answer us sincerely, and without   85
reserve; has Mr Marlow made you any professions of love
and affection?

MISS HARDCASTLE
The question is very abrupt, sir! But since you require unre-
served sincerity, I think he has.

HARDCASTLE (*To* SIR CHARLES)
You see.   90

SIR CHARLES
And pray, madam, have you and my son had more than
one interview?

MISS HARDCASTLE
Yes, sir, several.

HARDCASTLE (*To* SIR CHARLES)
  You see.
SIR CHARLES
  But did he profess any attachment?   95
MISS HARDCASTLE
  A lasting one.
SIR CHARLES
  Did he talk of love?
MISS HARDCASTLE
  Much, sir.
- SIR CHARLES
  Amazing! And all this formally?
MISS HARDCASTLE
  Formally.   100
HARDCASTLE
  Now, my friend, I hope you are satisfied.
SIR CHARLES
  And how did he behave, madam?
MISS HARDCASTLE
  As most professed admirers do. Said some civil things of my
  face, talked much of his want of merit, and the greatness of
  mine; mentioned his heart, gave a short tragedy speech, and 105
  ended with pretended rapture.
SIR CHARLES
  Now I'm perfectly convinced, indeed! I know his conversa-
  tion among women to be modest and submissive. This for-
  ward canting ranting manner by no means describes him,
  and I am confident he never sat for the picture.   110
MISS HARDCASTLE
  Then what, sir, if I should convince you to your face of my
  sincerity? If you and my papa, in about half an hour, will
  place yourselves behind that screen, you shall hear him
  declare his passion to me in person.
SIR CHARLES
  Agreed. And if I find him what you describe, all my happi- 115
  ness in him must have an end.   *Exit*
MISS HARDCASTLE
  And if you don't find him what I describe, – I fear my hap-
  piness must never have a beginning.

                                              Exeunt

109 *canting* hypocritical

[Act V, Scene ii]

Scene changes to the back of the garden

Enter HASTINGS

HASTINGS
What an idiot am I, to wait here for a fellow, who probably
takes a delight in mortifying me. He never intended to be
punctual, and I'll wait no longer. What do I see? It is he,
and perhaps with news of my Constance.

Enter TONY, *booted and spattered*

My honest Squire! I now find you a man of your word. This   5
looks like friendship.

TONY
Ay, I'm your friend, and the best friend you have in the
world, if you knew but all. This riding by night, by the bye,
is cursedly tiresome. It has shook me worse than the basket
of a stage-coach.   10

HASTINGS
But how? Where did you leave your fellow travellers? Are
they in safety? Are they housed?

TONY
Five and twenty miles in two hours and a half is no such
bad driving. The poor beasts have smoked for it: rabbit me,
but I'd rather ride forty miles after a fox, than ten with such   15
varment.

HASTINGS
Well, but where have you left the ladies? I die with impatience.

TONY
Left them! Why where should I leave them, but where I
found them?   20

HASTINGS
This is a riddle.

TONY
Riddle me this then. What's that goes round the house, and
round the house, and never touches the house?

HASTINGS
I'm still astray.

---

9 *basket* see note to I.i.11
14 *smoked* galloped
     rabbit me a mild oath, probably derived from 'God rot me' via 'rat me'
16 *varment* (Q italicises) vermin (colloquial) i.e. his mother and cousin

TONY

Why that's it, mon. I have led them astray. By jingo, there's   25
not a pond or slough within five miles of the place but they
can tell the taste of.

HASTINGS

Ha! ha! ha! I understand; you took them in a round, while
they supposed themselves going forward. And so you have
at last brought them home again.   30

TONY

You shall hear. I first took them down Featherbed Lane,
where we stuck fast in the mud. I then rattled them crack
over the stones of Up-and-down Hill. – I then introduced
them to the gibbet on Heavytree Heath, and from that, with
a circumbendibus, I fairly lodged them in the horsepond at   35
the bottom of the garden.

HASTINGS

But no accident, I hope?

TONY

No, no. Only mother is confoundedly frightened. She
thinks herself forty miles off. She's sick of the journey, and
the cattle can scarce crawl. So if your own horses be ready,   40
you may whip off with cousin, and I'll be bound that no
soul here can budge a foot to follow you.

HASTINGS

My dear friend, how can I be grateful?

TONY

Ay, now it's dear friend, noble Squire. Just now, it was all
idiot, cub, and run me through the guts. Damn *your* way of   45
fighting, I say. After we take a knock in this part of the
country, we kiss and be friends. But if you had run me
through the guts, then I should be dead, and you might go
kiss the hangman.

HASTINGS

The rebuke is just. But I must hasten to relieve Miss Neville;   50
if you keep the old lady employed, I promise to take care of
the young one.

TONY

Never fear me. Here she comes. Vanish.

Exit HASTINGS

---

25 *mon* man (Tony's pronunciation)
35 *circumbendibus* round-about way (mock-learned)
40 *cattle* horses (slang)
53 s.d. ed. (Q has it after Hastings's speech)

She's got from the pond, and draggled up to the waist like
a mermaid.   55

Enter MRS HARDCASTLE

MRS HARDCASTLE
Oh, Tony, I'm killed. Shook. Battered to death. I shall never
survive it. That last jolt, that laid us against the quickset
hedge, has done my business.
TONY
Alack, mamma, it was all your own fault. You would be for
running away by night, without knowing one inch of the   60
way.
MRS HARDCASTLE
I wish we were at home again. I never met so many acci-
dents in so short a journey. Drenched in the mud, over-
turned in a ditch, stuck fast in a slough, jolted to a jelly, and
at last to lose our way. Whereabouts do you think we are,   65
Tony?
TONY
By my guess we should be upon Crackskull Common,
about forty miles from home.
MRS HARDCASTLE
Oh lud! Oh lud! The most notorious spot in all the country.
We only want a robbery to make a complete night on't.   70
TONY
Don't be afraid, mamma, don't be afraid. Two of the five
that kept here are hanged, and the other three may not find
us. Don't be afraid. Is that a man that's galloping behind
us? No; it's only a tree. Don't be afraid.
MRS HARDCASTLE
The fright will certainly kill me.   75
TONY
Do you see anything like a black hat moving behind the
thicket?
MRS HARDCASTLE
Oh death!
TONY
No, it's only a cow. Don't be afraid, mamma; don't be
afraid.   80

---

54 *draggled* wet and slimy
57 *quickset* formed from living plants
58 *done my business* done for me
71–2 *five that kept here* i.e. highwaymen that worked here

MRS HARDCASTLE

As I'm alive, Tony, I see a man coming towards us. Ah! I'm
sure on't. If he perceives us we are undone.

TONY (*Aside*)

Father-in-law, by all that's unlucky, come to take one of his
night walks. (*To her*) Ah, it's a highwayman, with pistols as
long as my arm. A damned ill-looking fellow.   85

MRS HARDCASTLE

Good heaven defend us! He approaches.

TONY

Do you hide yourself in that thicket, and leave me to
manage him. If there be any danger I'll cough and cry hem!
When I cough be sure to keep close.

    MRS HARDCASTLE *hides behind a tree in the back scene*

Enter HARDCASTLE

HARDCASTLE

I'm mistaken, or I heard voices of people in want of help.   90
Oh, Tony, is that you? I did not expect you so soon back.
Are your mother and her charge in safety?

TONY

Very safe, sir, at my aunt Pedigree's. Hem!

MRS HARDCASTLE (*From behind*)

Ah death! I find there's danger.

HARDCASTLE

Forty miles in three hours; sure, that's too much, my young-   95
ster.

TONY

Stout horses and willing minds make short journeys, as they
say. Hem!

MRS HARDCASTLE (*From behind*)

Sure he'll do the dear boy no harm.

HARDCASTLE

But I heard a voice here; I should be glad to know from   100
whence it came?

TONY

It was I, sir, talking to myself, sir. I was saying that forty
miles in four hours was very good going. Hem! As to be

---

88 *cough and cry hem!* Othello orders Emilia to 'Cough, or cry hem, if anybody
    come' (*Othello*, IV.ii.31).

89 *close* hidden

89 s.d. *tree in the back scene* i.e. a tree painted on one of the wings, upstage; per-
    haps a mulberry (l. 133 below)

sure it was. Hem! I have got a sort of cold by being out in
the air. We'll go in, if you please. Hem!   105

HARDCASTLE

But if you talked to yourself, you did not answer yourself.
I am certain I heard two voices, and am resolved (*raising his
voice*) to find the other out.

MRS HARDCASTLE (*From behind*)

Oh! he's coming to find me out. Oh!

TONY

What need you go, sir, if I tell you? Hem! I'll lay down my   110
life for the truth – hem! – I'll tell you all, sir.

Detaining him

HARDCASTLE

I tell you, I will not be detained. I insist on seeing. It's in
vain to expect I'll believe you.

MRS HARDCASTLE (*Running forward from behind*)

Oh lud, he'll murder my poor boy, my darling. Here, good
gentleman, whet your rage upon me. Take my money, my   115
life, but spare that young gentleman, spare my child, if you
have any mercy.

HARDCASTLE

My wife, as I'm a Christian! From whence can she come, or
what does she mean?

MRS HARDCASTLE (*Kneeling*)

Take compassion on us, good Mr Highwayman. Take our   120
money, our watches, all we have, but spare our lives. We
will never bring you to justice, indeed we won't, good Mr
Highwayman.

HARDCASTLE

I believe the woman's out of her senses. What, Dorothy,
don't you know *me*?   125

MRS HARDCASTLE

Mr Hardcastle, as I'm alive. My fears blinded me. But who,
my dear, could have expected to meet you here, in this
frightful place, so far from home? What has brought you to
follow us?

HARDCASTLE

Sure, Dorothy, you have not lost your wits? So far from   130
home, when you are within forty yards of your own door?
(*To him*) This is one of your old tricks, you graceless rogue
you. (*To her*) Don't you know the gate, and the mulberry
tree; and don't you remember the horsepond, my dear?

110–11 *I'll lay down my life for the truth* Version of *vitam impendere vero* (Juvenal,
   Satires, IV, 91), the often-quoted motto of Rousseau.

MRS HARDCASTLE

    Yes, I shall remember the horsepond as long as I live; I have   135
caught my death in it. (*To* TONY) And is it to you, you
graceless varlet, I owe all this? I'll teach you to abuse your
mother, I will.

TONY

    Ecod, mother, all the parish says you have spoiled me, and
so you may take the fruits on't.   140

MRS HARDCASTLE

    I'll spoil you, I will!

Exit, driving TONY off the stage

HARDCASTLE

    There's morality, however, in his reply.   *Exit*

Enter HASTINGS and MISS NEVILLE

HASTINGS

    My dear Constance, why will you deliberate thus? If
we delay a moment, all is lost for ever. Pluck up a little
resolution, and we shall soon be out of the reach of her   145
malignity.

MISS NEVILLE

    I find it impossible. My spirits are so sunk with the agita-
tions I have suffered, that I am unable to face any new
danger. Two or three years' patience will at last crown us
with happiness.   150

HASTINGS

    Such a tedious delay is worse than inconstancy. Let us fly,
my charmer. Let us date our happiness from this very
moment. Perish fortune! Love and content will increase
what we possess beyond a monarch's revenue. Let me prevail.   155

MISS NEVILLE

    No, Mr Hastings; no. Prudence once more comes to my
relief, and I will obey its dictates. In the moment of passion,
fortune may be despised, but it ever produces a lasting
repentance. I'm resolved to apply to Mr Hardcastle's compassion and justice for redress.   160

HASTINGS

    But though he had the will, he has not the power to relieve
you.

MISS NEVILLE

    But he has influence, and upon that I am resolved to rely.

---

141 s.d. L (*Follows him off the stage. Exit.* Q)

HASTINGS
    I have no hopes. But since you persist, I must reluctantly
    obey you.   165

                                                        Exeunt

[Act V, Scene iii]

Scene changes [to HARDCASTLE's *house]*

Enter SIR CHARLES *and* MISS HARDCASTLE

SIR CHARLES
    What a situation I am in! If what you say appears, I shall
    then find a guilty son. If what he says be true, I shall then
    lose one that, of all others, I most wished for a daughter.
MISS HARDCASTLE
    I am proud of your approbation, and to show I merit it, if
    you place yourselves as I directed, you shall hear his explicit   5
    declaration. But he comes.
SIR CHARLES
    I'll to your father, and keep him to the appointment. *Exit*

                        Enter MARLOW

MARLOW
    Though prepared for setting out, I come once more to take
    leave, nor did I, till this moment, know the pain I feel in the
    separation.   10
MISS HARDCASTLE (*In her own natural manner*)
    I believe those sufferings cannot be very great, sir, which
    you can so easily remove. A day or two longer, perhaps
    might lessen your uneasiness, by showing the little value of
    what you now think proper to regret.
MARLOW (*Aside*)
    This girl every moment improves upon me. (*To her*) It must   15
    not be, madam. I have already trifled too long with my
    heart. My very pride begins to submit to my passion. The
    disparity of education and fortune, the anger of a parent,
    and the contempt of my equals, begin to lose their weight;
    and nothing can restore me to myself, but this painful effort   20
    of resolution.
MISS HARDCASTLE
    Then go, sir. I'll urge nothing more to detain you. Though
    my family be as good as hers you come down to visit, and

---

11 *those* L (these Q). Miss Hardcastle's natural manner allows such generalisations.

my education, I hope, not inferior, what are these advan-
tages without equal affluence? I must remain contented   25
with the slight approbation of imputed merit; I must have
only the mockery of your addresses, while all your serious
aims are fixed on fortune.

Enter HARDCASTLE *and* SIR CHARLES *from behind*

SIR CHARLES
Here, behind this screen.
HARDCASTLE
Ay, ay, make no noise. I'll engage my Kate covers him with   30
confusion at last.
MARLOW
By heavens, madam, fortune was ever my smallest con-
sideration. Your beauty at first caught my eye; for who
could see that without emotion. But every moment that I
converse with you, steals in some new grace, heightens the   35
picture, and gives it stronger expression. What at first
seemed rustic plainness, now appears refined simplicity.
What seemed forward assurance, now strikes me as the
result of courageous innocence, and conscious virtue.
SIR CHARLES
What can it mean? He amazes me!   40
HARDCASTLE
I told you how it would be. Hush!
MARLOW
I am now determined to stay, madam, and I have too good
an opinion of my father's discernment, when he sees you,
to doubt his approbation.
MISS HARDCASTLE
No, Mr Marlow, I will not, cannot detain you. Do you   45
think I could suffer a connexion, in which there is the
smallest room for repentance? Do you think I would take
the mean advantage of a transient passion, to load you with
confusion? Do you think I could ever relish that happiness,
which was acquired by lessening yours?   50
MARLOW
By all that's good, I can have no happiness but what's in
your power to grant me. Nor shall I ever feel repentance,
but in not having seen your merits before. I will stay, even
contrary to your wishes; and though you should persist to
shun me, I will make my respectful assiduities atone for the 55
levity of my past conduct.

28 s.d. *from behind* i.e. from behind the proscenium arch, onto the scenic stage
56 *conduct.* Q (conduct. / Sr Chas. I was never so confounded. / Hard. I told you

MISS HARDCASTLE

Sir, I must entreat you'll desist. As our acquaintance began,
so let it end, in indifference. I might have given an hour or
two to levity; but seriously, Mr Marlow, do you think I
could ever submit to a connexion, where *I* must appear   60
mercenary, and *you* imprudent? Do you think I could ever
catch at the confident addresses of a secure admirer?

MARLOW (*Kneeling*)

Does this look like security? Does this look like confidence?
No, madam, every moment that shows me your merit, only
serves to increase my diffidence and confusion. Here let me   65
continue –

SIR CHARLES

I can hold no longer. Charles, Charles, how hast thou
deceived me! Is this your indifference, your uninteresting
conversation?

HARDCASTLE

Your cold contempt; your formal interview. What have you   70
to say now?

MARLOW

That I'm all amazement! What can it mean?

HARDCASTLE

It means that you can say and unsay things at pleasure.
That you can address a lady in private, and deny it in
public; that you have one story for us, and another for my   75
daughter.

MARLOW

Daughter! – this lady your daughter!

HARDCASTLE

Yes, sir, my only daughter. My Kate, whose else should she
be?

MARLOW

Oh, the devil.   80

MISS HARDCASTLE

Yes, sir, that very identical tall squinting lady you were
pleased to take me for (*curtseying*). She that you addressed
as the mild, modest, sentimental man of gravity, and the

how it would be. Just now he'll deny every syllable of this to our faces. L). Q's
omission probably shows that this exchange was cut in performance; it largely
repeats ll. 40–1, and awkwardly interrupts the lovers' dialogue.

62 *catch* snatch
67 *hold* L (hold it Q): restrain myself (*OED* 27)
83 *gravity* Q (SPECULATION L)

bold, forward, agreeable Rattle of the Ladies' Club; ha! ha!
ha!   85
MARLOW
Zounds, there's no bearing this; it's worse than death.
MISS HARDCASTLE
In which of your characters, sir, will you give us leave to
address you? As the faltering gentleman, with looks on the
ground, that speaks just to be heard, and hates hypocrisy;
or the loud confident creature, that keeps it up with Mrs   90
Mantrap, and old Miss Biddy Buckskin, till three in the
morning; ha! ha! ha!
MARLOW
Oh, curse on my noisy head. I never attempted to be impu-
dent yet, that I was not taken down. I must be gone.
HARDCASTLE
By the hand of my body, but you shall not. I see it was all   95
a mistake, and I am rejoiced to find it. You shall not, sir, I
tell you. I know she'll forgive you. Won't you forgive him,
Kate? We'll all forgive you. Take courage, man.

They retire, she tormenting him, to the back scene

Enter MRS HARDCASTLE, TONY

MRS HARDCASTLE
So, so, they're gone off. Let them go, I care not.
HARDCASTLE
Who gone?   100
MRS HARDCASTLE
My dutiful niece and her gentleman, Mr Hastings, from
town. He who came down with our modest visitor here.
SIR CHARLES
Who, my honest George Hastings? As worthy a fellow as
lives, and the girl could not have made a more prudent
choice.   105
HARDCASTLE
Then, by the hand of my body, I'm proud of the connexion.
MRS HARDCASTLE
Well, if he has taken away the lady, he has not taken her
fortune; that remains in this family to console us for her
loss.

---

86 *death* Q, Bell, Inchbald, Cooke (a charg'd culverin L). Players perhaps felt that
   for Marlow to fear a loaded gun or cannon would be too unmanly.
89 *just to be heard* so as scarcely to be heard
93 *noisy* clamorous, making trouble
96 *not, sir* Q (not stir L)

HARDCASTLE

Sure Dorothy you would not be so mercenary?　　　110

MRS HARDCASTLE

Ay, that's my affair, not yours.

HARDCASTLE

But you know if your son, when of age, refuses to marry his cousin, her whole fortune is then at her own disposal.

MRS HARDCASTLE

Ay, but he's not of age, and she has not thought proper to wait for his refusal.　　　115

Enter HASTINGS *and* MISS NEVILLE

(*Aside*) What, returned so soon? I begin not to like it.

HASTINGS (*To* HARDCASTLE)

For my late attempt to fly off with your niece, let my present confusion be my punishment. We are now come back, to appeal from your justice to your humanity. By her father's consent, I first paid her my addresses, and our pas-　120
sions were first founded in duty.

MISS NEVILLE

Since his death, I have been obliged to stoop to dissimulation to avoid oppression. In an hour of levity, I was ready even to give up my fortune to secure my choice. But I'm now recovered from the delusion, and hope from your ten-　125
derness what is denied me from a nearer connexion.

MRS HARDCASTLE

Pshaw, pshaw, this is all but the whining end of a modern novel.

HARDCASTLE

Be it what it will, I'm glad they're come back to reclaim their due. Come hither, Tony boy. Do you refuse this lady's　130
hand whom I now offer you?

TONY

What signifies my refusing? You know I can't refuse her till I'm of age, father.

HARDCASTLE

While I thought concealing your age, boy, was likely to conduce to your improvement, I concurred with your　135
mother's desire to keep it secret. But since I find she turns it

---

112　s.p. HARDCASTLE L (Q adds this speech to the preceding one)

　of age of legal age, twenty-one; see I.i.33 and note, and ll.134–40 below.

114　s.p. MRS HARDCASTLE L (HARDCASTLE Q): Q is incorrect since Hardcastle knows Tony is of age and approves Miss Neville's choice.

127–8　The play's working-title had been 'The Novel'. Reviewers often complained that novels had sentimental happy endings; see *Works*, vol. I p. 206.

to a wrong use, I must now declare, you have been of age
these three months.

TONY

Of age! Am I of age, father?

HARDCASTLE

Above three months.   140

TONY

Then you'll see the first use I'll make of my liberty. (*Taking*
MISS NEVILLE'*s hand*) Witness all men by these presents,
that I, Anthony Lumpkin, Esquire, of BLANK place, refuse
you, Constantia Neville, spinster, of no place at all, for my
true and lawful wife. So Constance Neville may marry   145
whom she pleases, and Tony Lumpkin is his own man
again.

SIR CHARLES

Oh brave Squire!

HASTINGS

My worthy friend.

MRS HARDCASTLE

My undutiful offspring.   150

MARLOW

Joy, my dear George, I give you joy sincerely. And could I
prevail upon my little tyrant here to be less arbitrary, I
should be the happiest man alive, if you would return me
the favour.

HASTINGS (*To* MISS HARDCASTLE)

Come, madam, you are now driven to the very last scene of   155
all your contrivances. I know you like him, I'm sure he
loves you, and you must and shall have him.

HARDCASTLE (*Joining their hands*)

And I say so too. And Mr Marlow, if she makes as good a
wife as she has a daughter, I don't believe you'll ever repent
your bargain. So now to supper, tomorrow we shall gather   160
all the poor of the parish about us, and the mistakes of the
night shall be crowned with a merry morning; so, boy, take
her; and as you have been mistaken in the mistress, my wish
is, that you may never be mistaken in the wife.

FINIS

145–6 *Constance ... pleases* There was an old theatre tradition of saying 'Constance
    Neville may go to the devil'. A laugh may be had legitimately by keeping
    Goldsmith's words and pausing after 'Neville' and 'may'.

164 *FINIS* Q, L. No general *exeunt* is marked; probably all the players waited for the
    epilogue.

EPILOGUE

By DR GOLDSMITH

Well, having stooped to conquer with success,
And gained a husband without aid from dress,
Still as a barmaid, I could wish it too,
As I have conquered him to conquer you:
And let me say, for all your resolution,   5
That pretty barmaids have done execution.
Our life is all a play, composed to please,
'We have our exits and our entrances'.
The first act shows the simple country maid,
Harmless and young, of everything afraid;   10
Blushes when hired, and with unmeaning action,
'I hopes as how to give you satisfaction'.
Her second act displays a livelier scene –
The unblushing barmaid of a country inn.
Who whisks about the house, at market caters,   15
Talks loud, coquets the guests, and scolds the waiters.
Next the scene shifts to town, and there she soars,
The chop-house toast of ogling connoisseurs.
On squires and cits she there displays her arts,
And on the gridiron broils her lovers' hearts –   20
And as she smiles, her triumphs to complete,
Even Common Councilmen forget to eat.
The fourth act shows her wedded to the Squire,
And Madam now begins to hold it higher;
Pretends to taste, at operas cries *caro*,   25
And quits her Nancy Dawson, for *Che faro*.
Dotes upon dancing, and in all her pride,

0.1 *Epilogue* Spoken by Mrs Bulkely in the character of Miss Hardcastle.

6 *done execution* conquered or killed admirers; see l. 30 below.

8 Version of *As You Like It*, II.vii.141. The rest of the epilogue parodies Jacques's well-known 'seven ages of man' speech.

15 *caters* buys food

18 *chop-house* cheap cafe

19 *cits* tradesmen

22 *Common Councilmen* Councillors, especially in London

25 *caro* excellent (Italian)

26 *Nancy Dawson* a famous hornpipe dancer, who had a song named after her
Che faro a famous aria from Gluck's opera *Orfeo* (1764)

Swims round the room, the Heinel of Cheapside;
Ogles and leers with artificial skill,
Till having lost in age the power to kill   30
She sits all night at cards, and ogles at spadille.
Such, through our lives, the eventful history –
The fifth and last act still remains for me.
The barmaid now for your protection prays,
Turns female barrister, and pleads for Bayes.   35

28 *Heinel* Anna-Frederica Heinel, a famous ballet dancer
    Cheapside a London shopping street
31 *spadille* the ace of spades in the games of ombre and quadrille
35 *Bayes* Originally the laurel crown awarded to successful poets in ancient con-
    tests; the word had acquired the sense of poet or dramatist from the character of
    Bayes in Buckingham's *The Rehearsal*.

EPILOGUE*

By J. CRADOCK, Esq.

To be spoken in the character of TONY LUMPKIN

Well – now all's ended – and my comrades gone,
Pray what becomes of *mother's nonly son?*
A hopeful blade! – in town I'll fix my station,
And try to make a bluster in the nation.
As for my cousin Neville, I renounce her,   5
Off – in a crack – I'll carry the big Bet Bouncer.
    Why should not I in the great world appear?
I soon shall have a thousand pounds a year;
No matter what a man may here inherit,
In London – 'gad, they've some regard to spirit.   10
I see the horses prancing up the streets,
And big Bet Bouncer, bobs to all she meets;
Then hoikes to jigs and pastimes ev'ry night –
Not to the plays – they say it a'n't polite;
To Sadler's Wells perhaps, or operas go,   15
And once by chance, to the roratorio.
Thus here and there, for ever up and down,
We'll set the fashions too, to half the town;
And then at auctions – money ne'er regard,
Buy pictures like the great, ten pounds a yard;   20

0.2 CRADOCK Joseph Cradock, a dabbler in literature and friend of Goldsmith, had read the play in manuscript. Goldsmith thanked him for his epilogue, said it 'could not be used', and asked permission to print it. Longer versions were printed in *Lloyd's Evening Post*, 8–10 April 1773, and Cradock's *Literary Memoirs* (1826), Vol. I p. 226. See Balderston, pp. xxxviii–xl, 118–19, and Friedman, p. 88.

0.2–3 By ... LUMPKIN ed. (Q reverses the two lines)

2 *mother's nonly son* a Lumpkinism from an earlier version of the play, like 'roratorio', l. 16 below

13 *hoikes* hikes

14 *a'n't* ain't, isn't

15 *Sadler's Wells* theatre was not licensed for plays, but produced popular musical entertainments.

16 *roratorio* see note to l. 2 above. Oratorios were regularly performed in the London theatres.

Zounds, we shall make these London gentry say,
We know what's damned genteel, as well as they.

* This came too late to be spoken.

APPENDIX

Song intended for

She Stoops to Conquer

Ah me, when shall I marry me?
Lovers are plenty but fail to relieve me;
He, fond youth, that could carry me,
Offers to love but means to deceive me.

But I will rally and combat the ruiner;   5
Not a look, not a smile shall my passion discover;
She that gives all to the false one pursuing her
Makes but a penitent, loses a lover.

0.1 *Song* printed by Davis from the autograph manuscript in the Boswell papers at
Yale. Boswell published it in the June 1774 *London Magazine*, vol. xliii p. 295,
with a letter explaining that Goldsmith intended it for Miss Hardcastle, but it
was left out, as Mrs Bulkely was no singer. Mrs Abington, who had turned down
the role, was a ballad singer. Boswell had heard Goldsmith himself sing it to the
tune of 'The Humours of Balamagairy' (*Life of Johnson*, 13 April 1773). M.
Sands says this Irish air is also known as 'Old Langoler' (*Music and Letters* vol.
xxxii, 1951, p. 149). Miss Hardcastle's song fits in best at the very end of Act
III, when acting as barmaid she has found that she wants to marry Marlow, but
he only wants to seduce her.
3 *carry me* sweep me off my feet